THE GOSPEL OF JOHN
AND JUDAISM

THE GOSPEL OF JOHN
AND JUDAISM

C. K. BARRETT

Translated from the German by
D. M. SMITH

FORTRESS PRESS

Philadelphia

First published in German 1970
with the title Das Johannesevangelium und das Judentum
by Verlag W. Kohlhammer GmbH
Stuttgart and Berlin

© 1970 Verlag W. Kohlhammer GmbH

Translation © The Society for Promoting Christian Knowledge, 1975

First American Edition by Fortress Press 1975

Library of Congress Catalog Card Number 75-15435

ISBN 0-8006-0431-8

5113J75   Printed in the U.S.A.   1-431

Contents

Acknowledgements

Thanks are due to the following for permission to quote from copyright sources:

E. J. Brill, Leiden: *A Life of Rabban Yohanan ben Zakkai*, by J. Neusner.

Cambridge University Press: *The Interpretation of the Fourth Gospel*, by C. H. Dodd.

Doubleday and Co. Inc.: *The Gospel According to John*, by Raymond E. Brown.

Professor W. C. van Unnik: 'The Purpose of St. John's Gospel', *Studia Evangelica* 1 (Texte und Untersuchungen 73).

Biblical quotations from the Revised Standard Version of the Bible, copyrighted 1946, 1952, and 1957 by the Division of Christian Education of the National Council of the Churches of Christ in the United States of America, are used by permission.

Preface

This book contains the Franz Delitzsch Lectures for 1967, which I gave in December of that year in Münster. The lectures were delivered in the University under the auspices of the Institutum Judaicum Delitzschianum, and were published in German by W. Kohlhammer, of Stuttgart, with the title *Das Johannesevangelium und das Judentum* (1970). In the Preface to this German edition I expressed my gratitude for the honour conferred in the invitation to deliver the lectures, and for all the hospitality and kindness shown me by Professor K. H. Rengstorf, then Director of the Institutum Judaicum, and by his colleagues. Lapse of time has not dimmed my memory of the occasion or reduced my gratitude, and it is a pleasure to repeat my thanks here.

I wrote the lectures in German, my friend and colleague Dr K. H. Kuhn kindly helping me to make them reasonably idiomatic and free from error. After delivery they were further polished and prepared for the press by Professor Rengstorf and his assistant Dr W. Dietrich. It is at the suggestion of Professor D. M. Smith, of Duke University, that an English edition now appears, a suggestion which Professor Smith backed up by himself undertaking the translation, and I take this opportunity to express to him my admiring gratitude for the labour, both self-denying and efficient, that he has put into my book. The translation is his except that he has tolerated a number of suggestions from me, which, though they may not have improved his rendering of the German, have at least made the finished product rather more like what I would have said if I had written the lectures in English to begin with.

I am grateful also to the Verlag W. Kohlhammer, who have permitted the publication of this English version.

I have not attempted, in helping to prepare this English edition, to introduce more than one or two references to literature on the Fourth Gospel that has appeared between 1967 and 1973. Some points alluded to in the book I have myself taken up more fully, and may here refer to *The Prologue of St John's Gospel* (The Athlone Press of London University, London 1971; reprinted in *New Testament Essays* (S.P.C.K., London 1972), pp. 27–48); 'The Dialectical Theology of St John', in *New Testament Essays*, pp. 49–69; and ' "The Father is greater than I" (John 14.28): Subordinationist Christology in the New Testament', in *Neues Testament und Kirche, Festschrift für R. Schnackenburg* (Herder, Freiburg-Basel-Wien 1974), pp. 144–59. A few other books may be mentioned. *John and Qumran* (Geoffrey Chapman, London 1972), a volume of essays by various authors edited by J. H. Charlesworth, puts together a great deal of valuable Qumran material. J. L. Martyn's *History and Theology in the Fourth Gospel* (Harper and Row, New York and Evanston 1968) is an admirable discussion of the historical and theological setting of the gospel, not without points of contact with mine, though in some important respects his approach is different. In view of the discussion of Johannine topography on pp. 36ff. Professor Smith suggests to me that I should draw attention to W. D. Davies's *The Gospel and the Land* (University of California Press, Berkeley 1973). Unfortunately I have not yet seen a copy of this book, but I know some of my old friend's thoughts on the subject, and have no doubt that the book ought to be used by all students of the gospel.

This is the first book I have published with S.P.C.K. since

the death of its former Director, Dr Francis Noel Davey, and I cannot send it out without recording a sense of obligation that I shall never lose. It was in 1936 that I carried my first New Testament essay along Trumpington Street from Pembroke to his rooms in Corpus, and began an association that grew steadily in depth and in warmth. Information about the New Testament I had to collect for myself, but he more than anyone else helped me to see that to collect it, however great the labour, and to understand it, and the book itself, was the most responsible and rewarding task any scholar could undertake. He published my first book; and through the years a letter from him, the rare opportunity of conversation, have never failed to rekindle the flame. I can no longer thank him; but I am thankful to God for him.

Durham, January 1974   C. K. BARRETT

1

The Environment and Purpose
of the Fourth Gospel

No one can satisfactorily explain a text if he has no knowledge of its environment, the readership for which it was
intended, and the purpose for which it was written. If a book
is anonymous, published without notice and review, there is
likewise no means of investigating its environment, readership, and purpose, and thus of explaining it. This dilemma
is nothing new for the student of ancient literature. Nor has
it only recently been discovered that there is no ancient
book in which the problem is more acute or bewildering than
it is in the Fourth Gospel. Doubtless this fact has contributed
to a situation in which fashions in exegesis and in the identification of the purpose and environment of this gospel have
changed so frequently and so radically. All this is well
known, so that a few brief examples will suffice to illustrate
the state in which we find ourselves.

An Englishman may perhaps be pardoned if he begins
with Westcott.[1] In his argument that the Gospel was written
by John the Son of Zebedee the first steps are (a) the proof
that the author was a Jew and (b) the proof that he was a
Palestinian Jew. He must be sharply distinguished from a
Hellenistic Jew such as Philo. 'The teaching of St John is
characteristically Hebraic and not Alexandrine.'[2] In the
early years of the twentieth century the same point of view
was also advocated by Drummond[3] and Sanday.[4] But

already in England, if somewhat later than in Germany, scholarship was taking a new turn. Moffatt represents the later viewpoint when he writes: 'Apart from the Old Testament, the main currents which flow through the gospel are those of (*a*) Paulinism, (*b*) the Jewish Alexandrian philosophy, and (*c*) Stoicism.'[5] Concerning the purpose of the gospel he maintains:

> The Fourth Gospel represents the first serious attempt to re-state the primitive faith for some wider circles who were susceptible to Hellenic influences, and the author, in translating the gospel of Jesus for their benefit, shows himself a master not only in his selection of the matter he had to convey, but in his grasp of the language in which he had to reproduce his beliefs.[6]

Moffatt's standpoint was essentially pragmatic in that it was grounded upon exegetical observations rather than upon systematic considerations and wider questions. In this he differed from the position of A. Schweitzer,[7] who began with the problem of how the eschatological preaching of Jesus developed further in the second century. In Schweitzer's view it was not Paul who hellenized the eschatological message of early Christianity; rather he gave this message a form in which it could be hellenized. 'The Hellenistic conception of redemption through union with Christ is set forth with admirable completeness in the Gospel of John.'[8] 'The general attitude in the Gospel of John is the same as in Justin's *Dialogue with Trypho*. It reflects the struggle with which Christianity freed itself from the Judaism which began, after the destruction of Jerusalem, to close itself against the outside world.'[9]

The question of the background of Johannine thought—Jewish or Greek?—was investigated further by C. H. Dodd, yet the result was not essentially different. In the first part of his book on the interpretation of the Fourth Gospel[10] he dealt with the situation in early Christianity, the Hermetic literature, Hellenistic Judaism (particularly Philo of Alexandria), Gnosticism, and Mandaism. He regarded Mandaism as unimportant except as it contributes to our knowledge of Gnosticism. Gnosticism he defined as 'a label for a large and somewhat amorphous group of religious systems described by Irenaeus and Hippolytus in their works against Heresy . . . and similar systems known from other sources'.[11] This Gnosticism shares a common environment with Johannine Christianity. Yet the latter is 'an entirely different thing from semi-Christian or near-Christian Gnosticism'.[12] Rabbinic Judaism is another matter. Dodd singles out a number of parallels, which he regards as important. Yet in his discussion of Johannine Christology he says: 'The positive and significant elements in the Johannine Christology find little or no point of attachment to Jewish messianic ideas.'[13] The most significant parallels are to be found in Philo and in the Hermetic literature. By means of these parallels, which are in part the antitheses of Johannine statements, Dodd lays bare the most important Christian characteristics of the gospel. The Fourth Gospel 'certainly presupposes a range of ideas having a remarkable resemblance to those of Hellenistic Judaism as represented by Philo'.[14] Moreover, he maintains: 'As a whole they [the Hermetic writings] represent a type of religious thought akin to one side of Johannine thought.'[15] On the basis of these observations Dodd comes to the following conclusion: 'We are to think of the work as addressed to a wide public consisting primarily of devout and thoughtful persons . . . in the varied and cosmopolitan society of a great Hellenistic city such as Ephesus under the Roman Empire.'[16] Therefore the gospel is, in spite of its Jewish origin, a Hellenistic work in the sense that it is addressed to a Hellenistic audience.

Two ways of treating the problem of the Johannine world which in different ways avoid the direct question of whether it was Jewish or Greek must now be mentioned. That these approaches can be so described does not mean that they may be dismissed as unimportant. On the contrary, they are among the most important contributions to the debate. Even if I do not mention them frequently, they nevertheless lie directly under the surface of the discussion.

The first approach attempts to explain the Johannine litera-ture within the Bible and the Christian tradition and with-out reference to non-Christian influences. Here especially the work of E. C. Hoskyns[17] must be taken into account. (R. H. Lightfoot[18] follows a somewhat similar line.) The editor, F. N. Davey, appropriately summarized Hoskyns' posthum-ously published book when he wrote as follows concerning the danger of identifying the gospel with some part of its environment: This environment is admittedly manifold. 'Very probably [the evangelist] knew one or more of [the synoptic] gospels in their extant form. In addition, his thought bears the marks of a wide knowledge of the Old Testament Scriptures, while the Odes of Solomon as well as the rabbinic writings seem to throw light upon his work. Nor can Greek thought be excluded from his formative background, nor yet the religious manner of thought of Oriental mysticism.'[19] Davey added: 'The danger is entirely obviated when it is recognized that what chiefly conditions the apprehension of the fourth Evangelist is a truly Biblical realism.'[20] Hoskyns himself can also be cited in the same sense with reference to the term λόγος:

> The texture of the prologue is taken from the Old Testament Scriptures (e.g. Gen. 1; Prov. 8); but it is altogether Christian. That Jesus once spoke is more fundamental for its understand-ing than is the history of Greek philosophy or the story of the westward progress of Oriental mysticism; more fundamental even than the first chapter of Genesis or the eighth chapter of the Proverbs.[21]

This means that in the final analysis the gospel explains itself, and there is surely a sense in which this is so. The critical scholar may not forget that for many centuries men both ignorant and educated, who knew nothing about Alexandrian Judaism, have read the Fourth Gospel and heard in it the word of God. One must also concede that dual images such as Father–Son, Light–Darkness, and Life–Death possess a universal quality which is not dependent upon a particular environment. Rather they are generally understandable because of their basis in the common experiences of life. One must also recognize that the Fourth Gospel is essentially a biblical book, a book which stands within the biblical tradition and requires for its understanding those same presuppositions one discovers in the reading of Isaiah, Mark, Romans, and the like. All this is true; yet one may doubt whether it suffices for an adequate treatment of our subject.

It has been said that Hoskyns has done for John's gospel in the English-speaking world what Barth did for Romans in the German.[22] (This is not far from the truth, and it is regrettable that Hoskyns' commentary on John has in this regard never found the recognition it deserves.) The comparison between Barth and Hoskyns brings to mind Barth's own description of Calvin and Calvin's commentaries: 'How energetically Calvin, having first established what stands in the text, sets himself to re-think the whole material and to wrestle with it, till the walls which separate the sixteenth century from the first become transparent! Paul speaks, and the man of the sixteenth century hears.'[23] That is surely the goal that Hoskyns sets for himself. Yet he has not fully attained it, perhaps because he died before the book was completed, but perhaps also because his methods were not radical enough. In the foreword of one of the later editions of his Romans commentary, Barth wrote: 'I do not wish to engage in a controversy with Bultmann as to which of us is the more radical. But I must go farther than he does and say that there are in the Epistle no words at all which are not words of those "other spirits" which he calls Jewish or

Popular Christian or Hellenistic or whatever else they may be.'[24] It seems to me that we, just when we study and observe these 'other spirits' as they pass through the hands of an author, come to know not only the personal faith of the author, but also the creative power of the New Testament. The word of God is no separable essence which stands alongside the human word and can be abstracted from it. Rather, it is alive and active; it permeates the human words and is clothed with them. Exegesis demands an analysis of this permeation. It is precisely Hoskyns' failure to undertake this analytical task that is the greatest weakness of his commentary.

This criticism of Hoskyns—and I should like here to acknowledge the great debt I owe to him, and to his editor—has led me into a digression. There is no cause for regret, however, for it actually represents a defence of these lectures. It shows that the investigation of the relation between the Fourth Gospel and Judaism is in no sense pure antiquarianism, but a necessary element of exegesis, and, indeed, of practical exegesis.

I return now to the main line of the lecture and take up the second of the two treatments of the Johannine world which I mentioned earlier. This is the commentary of Bultmann,[25] according to whose opinion the Johannine literature and theology is neither Greek nor Jewish, but Gnostic. Certainly there are connections with both Judaism and the Greek world. If, however, 'the author's background was Judaism, as rather frequently occurring rabbinical turns of speech perhaps prove, it was, at any rate, not out of an orthodox but out of a gnosticizing Judaism that he came'.[26] No one can deny that λόγος is a Greek word; yet 'out of Gnostic language, finally, and not as some maintain, out of the Greek philosophical tradition comes the pre-existent Revealer's name: Logos'.[27] Bultmann's definitions of the terms Gnosis and Gnosticism[28] are different from those of

Dodd, and the distinction is important. Bultmann writes: 'Gnosticism [German, *Gnosis*] is the name given to a phenomenon which appears in a variety of forms, but always with the same fundamental structure.' This phenomenon was 'a religious movement of pre-Christian origin, invading the West from the Orient as a competitor of Christianity . . . In general, we may call it a redemptive religion based on dualism.'[29] The historical question, which has arisen in the wake of Bultmann's deservedly famous work, is this: What are the sources on the basis of which we know this Gnosis, which John is supposed to have reworked? Are they not all post-Christian, and are not some of them very late?[30] To this question the answer is essentially as follows: The sources are indeed later than John; but the gospel becomes much more intelligible if one may suppose that there already existed a religion of that sort, although it can only be observed in later sources. Whether this argument is justified cannot be discussed here; in any case the question has not been settled. At this stage I should like only to point out that by a new route we have returned to the position of Hoskyns: The gospel is to be explained on its own terms. According to Bultmann's procedure the gospel seems to be a Christianizing of oriental Gnosis. Thus one first uses the gospel in order to reconstruct the Gnosis, and then uses the Gnosis to explain the gospel, in that one describes the reworking of this Gnosis by the evangelist. This method is not necessarily wrong, but it is dangerous. It can be called *Religionsgeschichte*, but it is *Religionsgeschichte* of a distinct sort, since the history (*Geschichte*) is produced, so to speak, only internally and not objectively.

During recent decades two circumstances have led to a strong reiteration of the Jewish background and origin of the gospel: on the one hand, the criticism, directed against Bultmann and those who follow him, concerning the relative lateness of the comparative material used to establish a

Gnostic background of John; on the other, and more important, the discovery of the Qumran scrolls. So, for example, W. Michaelis[31] writes: 'It may now be said that the Palestinian character of the Gospel of John has become so clear that attempts to promote another provenance really should cease.' Here too is an hypothesis which we must investigate more thoroughly later. The question pertains not only to the origin of the gospel, but also to its purpose: For what readers and to what purpose was it written?

There are also more recent efforts to answer this question which we must examine. In several respects they have given the discussion a new direction. The most important was made by W. C. van Unnik in a paper presented to the Oxford Congress on the Gospels of 1957.[32]

Taking his start from John 20.30f (ταῦτα δὲ γέγραπται ἵνα πιστεύητε ὅτι Ἰησοῦς ἐστιν ὁ χριστὸς ὁ υἱὸς τοῦ θεοῦ) van Unnik maintained that the various purposes ascribed to John could be summarized under three heads:

(a) John wrote for non-Christians. According to this opinion his gospel is a missionary tract intended for the earnest and reflective pagan. Such people would consider the claims of a new spiritual religion if only they were expressed in a language they could understand, that is, not in Jewish, but in Hellenistic forms of speech.

(b) John was written for Christians in order to mediate to them a deeper understanding of their faith. Therefore, the gospel would perhaps be a landmark of the expansion of the Church into a new environment, or perhaps an answer to the problems of eschatology and Gnosis, which were urgent matters for the Church at the end of the first century.

(c) John undertook a counterattack against the Jews, who were defaming the Christian Messiah. Therefore, John would be a precursor of Justin's *Dialogue with Trypho*. His purpose would not have been historical, but polemical, and his work would then reflect debates with Diaspora Jews.

Van Unnik asks: Have not scholars who represent these viewpoints neglected to take John 20.30 of seriously? It is noteworthy (already Westcott noted the same error in the works of his predecessors and contemporaries) that these verses have at times been erroneously cited, in that the term 'Christ' actually falls out and the title 'Son of God' is thus stressed. He goes on to ask: Can it really be satisfactory to maintain that John presents Jesus in the role of a Gnostic revealer when the evangelist himself explains that Jesus is the Christ—the Messiah—and the Son of God? The faith that John commends, that Jesus is the Messiah, must be regarded as especially important and noteworthy. John, alone among the evangelists, retains the transliterated term Μεσσίας and explains it (1.41). 'Messiah' does not mean 'Christ', which would only be a new name in another language, but the 'anointed'. Thus John understands 'Messiah' in its full and proper sense. For John (although he could use the term 'King of the Jews') the Messiah was more a universal than a national figure; that does not mean, however, that John did not know the Jewish, nationalistic roots of his universal concept. On the contrary, 6.15 and 12.13 show that he was entirely familiar with them. After the year 70 there were good grounds to omit such dangerous and seemingly anti-Roman expressions. John does not, however, omit them, but includes them in places where they are not found in the synoptics. This corroborates the view that for John 'the "Anointed King of Israel" was a living title and not just an empty shell'.[33]

The next step in van Unnik's line of argument proceeds from the Johannine assertion that Jesus is the Christ and

attempts to determine the *Sitz im Leben* of this thesis. The
thesis is found also in Acts (9.20, 22; 17.2, 3; 18.5, 28). This
indicates—for there is no reason to mistrust the Lucan
account—that the assertion in question had its setting in
Christian preaching and debates within the Diaspora synagogue. The historical development confirms this state of
affairs. Bar Cocheba had executed those Christians who
refused to deny that Jesus was the Messiah,[34] and Justin
made this belief the principal point of his dialogue with
Trypho.[35] With respect to the gospel, it is noteworthy that
the debates between Jesus and the Jews reflect a similar
interest. They are like a legal process in which the question
of whether or not Jesus is the Messiah is adjudicated.
Actually, these debates are not only similar to such a process. They are themselves such a process, and this process
must have gone on in the synagogue. The characteristically
Johannine term μαρτυρεῖν (and related words) belongs to
this setting, as does the term σημεῖον. The 'works are proof
of Jesus' Messiahship'.[36] The parallel designation of 'Son of
God' in John 20.30f is to be similarly explained (cf. Ps. 2.7;
2 Sam. 7.14).

What consequences concerning the environment of the
gospel and the purpose of the evangelist may be drawn from
these observations? Whether or not Jesus was the Messiah
would, by the very nature of the case, be a question appropriate to Palestine. Thus, 'the whole background of this gospel
is packed with Palestinian stories and conceptions; it smells
of the soil of Palestine. And yet there is also much that is
strange to Palestine.'[37] From this last observation it follows
that the synagogue in which the Johannine gospel was proclaimed, in which the Johannine debates took place, and
from which the Johannine Christians had been excluded
(9.22; 16.2) was the Diaspora synagogue. That this inference
is warranted is confirmed by the explanation of Palestinian
customs, the use of Greek expressions, and the concern for

the Diaspora (10.16; 11.52). One must also take account of
the interest in a Greek environment which emerges in 7.35
and 12.20. (On the distinction between Palestinian and
Diaspora Judaism, cf. Acts 13.26f).

Such considerations point to a conclusion which can best
be summarized in van Unnik's own words:

> The purpose of the Fourth Gospel was to bring the visitors of
> a synagogue in the Diaspora (Jews and Godfearers) to belief
> in Jesus as the Messiah of Israel. Thus we have found the
> 'Sitz im Leben' of this puzzling book and it appears not to be so
> isolated as it has often been thought. It was a missionary book
> for the Jews.... John did not write for Christians in the first
> place, except perhaps in chs. 13–17 which show a somewhat
> different character, nor did he envisage pagan readers. His
> book was not an apology to defend the Christian church, but a
> mission-book which sought to win. For this purpose: to make
> clear that Jesus is the Messiah, he worked over the material he
> had received.[38]

J. A. T. Robinson has argued similarly,[39] although he
reaches his conclusion along other paths. In Robinson's view
pagans are given little consideration in this gospel. The
Greeks who come to the feast to worship (12.20) are not
pagans, but Greek-speaking Jews; it was such men who
formed the groups with which John was concerned. In
John's view Jesus was the Messiah, and in his person represented the true Israel of God—as Manna, Light, Shepherd,
and Vine. The goal of John was to prevent Greek-speaking
Judaism from repeating the error of Palestinian Judaism in
rejecting Jesus. He hopes rather that both parts of Judaism
will become one in Christ (10.16; 11.52; 17.21), and that
thereafter—on the basis of this oneness—the rest of the world,
that is the non-Jewish world, will believe (17.21). The gospel
belongs to the world of Hellenistic Judaism. Yet John differs
from Philo; 'Philo was commending Judaism to Greek-
speaking paganism: John was commending Christianity to

Greek-speaking Judaism.'[40] Again I can best summarize in the words of the author himself. The gospel

> is composed . . . of material which took shape as teaching *within* a Christian community *in Judea* and under the pressure of controversy with 'the Jews' of that area. But in its present form it is . . . an appeal to those *outside* the Church, to win to the faith that Greek-speaking *Diaspora Judaism* to which the author now finds himself belonging as a result (we may surmise) of the greatest dispersion of all, which has swept from Judea Church and Synagogue alike.[41]

Therefore, for Robinson, as for van Unnik, the gospel is a Jewish book, Jewish in origin as well as in purpose.

I mentioned earlier the discovery of the Qumran scrolls. This discovery generated an impulse which has allowed the pendulum of Johannine scholarship to swing from a concentration upon Greek or non-Jewish influences back to the Jewish side. Later, I must say more about this matter and draw a brief comparison between the gospel and the Qumran texts. But in the framework of this brief survey of contemporary efforts to see the gospel in its original setting and to understand its original purpose, it is necessary to mention only the works of those scholars who have postulated not only a theological and religious relationship, but historical connections between Johannine Christianity and the Qumran community. Among the best known of these scholars is O. Cullmann.[42]

In summary, and not wholly satisfactory, fashion[43] Cullmann explains the theological and cultic similarities between the Qumran community and the early church and asks how one can make intelligible 'the simultaneous close relationship and basic difference between the two movements'.[44] He notes answers to these questions which he regards as unsatisfactory and proposes to find the missing link in the Hellenists of Acts 6. They had very early formed a distinct group within Christianity. For although they have been regarded as

Palestinian rather than Diaspora Jews, they were 'the real founders of Christian missions'.[45] They were driven from Jerusalem because they, like the Essenes, 'rejected Temple worship'.[46] Their name, Ἑλληνισταί, is based on a verb that means not 'to speak Greek', but 'to live according to the Greek manner'—and that could indicate that they exhibited 'tendencies, more or less esoteric, and of a syncretistic origin'.[47] That John had a relation to these people is shown by John 4.38; this verse plays upon the fact mentioned in Acts 8, namely, that the Samaritans were evangelized by the Hellenists and not by the Apostles. Since there are clear parallels between John and the Qumran literature, we may draw a twofold conclusion—there was a connection between John and the Hellenists as well as between John and the Qumran sect. Opposition to the temple worship was the one thing common to all three groups—therefore the Johannine assertion that the dwelling place (σκηνή—שכינה; 1.14) of the Logos was no longer the temple, but the historical figure of Jesus, whose body took the place of the temple made with hands (2.19), and who himself took the place of Bethel, the holy place where angels moved between heaven and earth (1.51). Therefore John is interested also in Christian worship, and the Christian sacraments, which are to take the place of the old Jewish calendar of feasts. Therefore he also uses the Son of man title.

I should like to underline the importance of these investigations which have been undertaken by van Unnik, Robinson, Cullmann, and many others. It seems to me impossible, however, to accept all their conclusions. Nevertheless, they have put us in their debt, in that they have made us alert to a large sphere of ancient life and thought. This sphere is now accessible as never before to systematic study. It has never been doubted that the Fourth Gospel stands in a certain relation to Judaism. That has been recognized even by those who stress its Greek and Gnostic elements. But what

specifically constitutes this relation? And, more precisely, to
what form of Judaism is the Fourth Gospel related? These
are the principal questions with which these lectures must
deal, and later they must be studied in detail. The gospel was
written towards the end of the first century.[48] We must therefore seek to understand as much as possible about the Judaism
of this period. The Judaism of the time of Herod the Great
and the Judaism after Bar Cocheba will not prove so fruitful
for our particular investigation. Certainly it is possible, as
has often been maintained, to interpret John in the light of
Philo of Alexandria. Philo was active until A.D. 40; John
wrote about a half century later. Chronologically, it is
possible that John had read the books of Philo. But in the
opinion of most scholars this is unlikely, for direct literary
connections between John and Philo cannot be demon-
strated. Moreover, it is somewhat hazardous to suppose that
a way of thinking which can be documented for Alexandria
at the beginning of the century was also known in Ephesus
near its end.[49] Having said that, however, I do not wish to
maintain that Philo is of no importance for the study of the
Fourth Gospel; I wish only to exercise appropriate caution.
The rabbinic literature must be similarly evaluated. Not to
use it would be nonsensical; it is most important to compare
it with the Fourth Gospel. Yet the problem of chronology
must always be considered. What do we actually learn from
the rabbinic literature about the Judaism of the 80s and 90s?

Because Philo is a half-century earlier than John and the
rabbinic literature at least a whole century later, it is therefore all the more important to consider the newer sources. I
shall not go into the question of the exact date of the Qumran
scrolls. This question has been, and still is, the subject of
considerable discussion among specialists, and I do not
belong to their number. It suffices to say—and one can say it
with certainty—that the scrolls were treasured and author-
ized scriptures of a community which existed until the col-

lapse of the year 70. With that year, however, we have not yet arrived at the period in which the gospel was written and in which, as we shall later see,[50] the loss of the temple altered the circumstances, and in part also the character, of both Judaism and Christianity. Yet the period of the Qumran community was not far distant from the time when the gospel was composed. Accordingly, the Qumran scrolls are especially useful. A relation between Qumran and Gnosis has often been observed.[51] It has also been maintained that there was a certain historical connection between the remnants of the Qumran community and Jewish Christianity, which also bore Gnostic traces.[52] On these grounds one may also infer the significance of the newly discovered Gnostic sources for our discussion.

At almost the same time as the discovery of the scrolls from the Dead Sea, there was found in Nag Hammadi a Gnostic library, which has substantially enlarged and enhanced our knowledge of the early development of Gnosticism.[53] Many details remain unclear, yet it is becoming increasingly evident that there was at the end of the first Christian century a multifarious religious phenomenon in which Judaism, Christianity, and Gnosis played fluctuating roles. This amalgam and this fluctuation must be seriously considered in the investigation of the Fourth Gospel.

All this is said programmatically at this point. So far as possible we shall discuss these questions later. Now we return to the recent attempts to relate the Gospel of John to Judaism.

Van Unnik has convincingly shown that John held Jesus to be the Messiah, in whom the hopes and promises of the Old Testament had been fulfilled. Concerning him Moses had written in the law and the prophets (1.45), and the purpose of the gospel consists in the proof that he was the Christ, the Son of God. It is, however, noteworthy that in 20.31 the two titles, Messiah and Son of God, are placed side by side. Van Unnik says, rightly, that Son of God was originally a messianic title, that is, the title signified the inclusion of the Davidic family as a whole in the plan of God (2 Sam. 7.14), and the consequential inclusion of each king, and *a fortiori* of the anointed King of the last days, in the family of God (Ps. 2.7). Neither in the allegedly historical context of 2 Sam. 7 nor in the liturgical context of Ps. 2 does 'Son of God' indicate some metaphysical relationship to God. It is, however, undeniable that John presupposes such a relationship. ὁ μονογενὴς υἱὸς ὁ ὢν εἰς τὸν κόλπον τοῦ πατρός[54] must be one who shares the Father's mode of being. Especially important is the discussion of Sonship found in John 5. This discussion has almost no connection with the usual doctrine of the Messiah. Its starting-point (5.18) is the Jewish complaint that if Jesus calls God his own father, he is ἴσον ἑαυτὸν ποιῶν τῷ θεῷ (cf. 19.7). This complaint (like others in this gospel) is at once both invalid and valid. Jesus is like the Father, for he and the Father are one (10.30). This equality is, however, of such a sort that Jesus can also say that the Father is greater than he (14.28); for strictly speaking it is not he, the Son, who has made himself like the Father, but the Father who made him like himself. That is clearly set forth in John 5. The Son does nothing of himself (and is in this respect subordinate to the Father). He can only do what he sees the Father do (5.19). But he sees everything the Father does and he does everything he sees. In that respect he is like the Father, an equally divine agent of equally divine works (5.20). For example, only God can raise the dead, but God the Son shares this divine activity with God the Father (5.21). Moreover, the Father has relinquished his right to hold judgement and given it over to the Son (5.22). From this subordination arises their equality, which is the consequence of the decision and deed of the Father. The purpose is that all should honour the Son as the Father. To fail to honour the Son, who is sent, means to fail to honour the Father, who sent him (5.23). We cannot now discuss the origin of these concepts. It may only be said in brief that the concept of sending can be Gnostic; normally, however, we do not find it in the usual messianic idea. We are not here dealing with a fictional adoption of a human king into a divine family, an adoption which was fundamentally a political device intended to make the right of succession secure. Rather, one is sent to earth who is in essence and origin God.[55] Therefore, John 20.30f does not mean '. . . in order that you may believe that Jesus is the Christ, that is, the Son of God' (in the simple, messianic sense), but '. . . in order that you may believe that Jesus is the Christ (the recognized title of the early Christian tradition), and acknowledge that this title signifies that he is nothing less than the divine Son of God, who has come down from heaven as the redeemer with divine authority'.

It is scarcely necessary to add that this interpretation is confirmed by the following clause: '. . . that you may have life in his name'. The Johannine use of 'eternal life' need not be discussed here. One may, however, say without qualification that life in the Johannine sense is something that no ordinary Messiah can give; it can only be understood as the gift of a supernatural redeemer.

Now we can make a further observation. The purpose clause 'that you may believe' cannot prove that John wrote either to strengthen the faith of Christians or to win non-Christians.[56] But if one recalls that John challenges his readers to believe that Jesus is the Christ, and that in the sense that he is the Son of God, it then becomes probable that his purpose consists in setting forth the full significance of an already existing Christian faith. John wrote not for pagans, not for Jews, but for Christians. This conclusion becomes even more convincing if one recalls the foregoing section. There the climax lies in the confession of Thomas: My Lord and my God. Did John then go on to write: Yes, that is what Thomas said; but I, John, ask you to believe only this, that Jesus is the messianic King of Israel, to whom God proffered an honour which he was to share with David and many others of his family line? If one is to see in 20.31 the climax of the whole gospel, the verse cannot mean less than 20.28.

The reference to the synagogue ban in 9.22; 16.2 can scarcely prove that the gospel was intended only, or in the first instance, for Jews in the Diaspora. Doubtless it is true that the evangelist knew of such a ban. Probably he knew Christians who were also Jews and who, as Jews, had suffered under this ban. That suffices to explain chapter 9. This chapter reflects a situation which lies wholly within a Jewish frame of reference. The threat against the parents of the man born blind, who fear to confess Christ, is correspondingly described. Also in chapter 16 the words are directed to Jews, namely to the first disciples of Jesus. The dangerous situation of such Jewish Christians must also have been known to their non-Jewish fellow-Christians.[57] The whole context places the hatred of the world in a broad framework, but it is not surprising that John, in a purportedly historical work, gave this hatred an appropriate (Jewish) form.

The argument that the Ἕλληνες in 12.20 are not Greeks or pagans but Jews of the Diaspora is not convincing. Linguistically this interpretation is not tenable, as Bauer[58] and Windisch[59] have already shown. These Ἕλληνες are most naturally Greeks who are interested in the culture and religion of Judaism. Strathmann has accurately described them:

> The men with whom we are concerned are not Hellenists, i.e. Greek-speaking Jews . . ., but 'Hellenes', people from the Greek-speaking world. Admittedly, they have sufficient interest in the religion of Israel to take the trouble to travel to Jerusalem in order to participate in the Passover Feast. Therefore, they are God-fearing Greeks, . . . proselytes, though not in the strictest sense, that is, without having been required to receive circumcision.[60]

This is confirmed not only by the most probable interpretation of 7.35 (εἰς τὴν διασπορὰν τῶν Ἑλλήνων . . . διδάσκειν τοὺς Ἕλληνας), but also by the context of 12.20. Without question this is presented as a climax of the gospel. When Jesus hears the report concerning the Greeks, he explains: ἐλήλυθεν ἡ ὥρα ἵνα δοξασθῇ ὁ υἱὸς τοῦ ἀνθρώπου, and with the help of the image of the kernel of wheat predicts his death. The latter is the presupposition of the world-wide expansion of the Gospel. A voice from heaven speaks, and Jesus underlines the turning point which has just occurred: Now is the judgement of the world; now is the ruler of this world cast out. And he adds the prophecy: I, if I am lifted up from the earth, will draw all men to myself.[61]

It seems to me impossible to accept the hypothesis that the Fourth Gospel is a missionary tract for the Judaism of the Diaspora. This does not mean that it is perverse of van Unnik and Robinson to emphasize the Jewish cast of the argumentation and motivation of the gospel, but the gospel has also Hellenistic and Gnostic connections, and cannot therefore be satisfactorily understood or interpreted within a Jewish context alone, even within the context of Qumran. Precisely the Jewish element in the gospel is not adequately understood if it is observed in isolation. This Jewish element exists not only because the gospel purports to recount the life of a Jew, Jesus of Nazareth, and not only because the evangelist has drawn upon Jewish sources. The composition of the book itself took place in a setting which was partly, but only partly, Jewish. The person who published the book in the form in which we read it today lived in Jewish circles, if at the same time in other circles also. The question which the gospel raises, and with which I shall deal in these lectures is not, Does the gospel come into contact with Judaism?, but To what sort of Judaism is the gospel related, and how may we understand the relation? Judaism is a broad concept; Johannine Judaism, however, requires a narrower definition.

2

Language and Provenance of
the Fourth Gospel

In this second lecture I should like to deal with a special problem area, without, however, forgetting the purpose indicated above (p. 19). That may certainly be less interesting than the setting forth of far-reaching hypotheses that are supposed to illumine the entire Gospel of John and its setting. Yet small matters of detail are of the greatest importance, since they contribute to the solution of the major questions.

I shall deal first with the question of the language of the Fourth Gospel. In our New Testament the Fourth Gospel lies before us as a Greek book. Is that its original form? Was the gospel, or were some of its parts, originally written in Aramaic? Or—if a translation hypothesis seems too bold—was the author, or the author of one of the sources, or the editor who put the sources together, a Jew who wrote in Greek but thought in Aramaic? Semitizing writing can naturally be explained in other ways; one could, for example, think of a conscious imitation of the style of the Septuagint. But the varieties of Semitisms which I have mentioned are those which have been most frequently discovered in the Gospel of John, for the questions which I have just raised are in no way new.

The history of the investigation of the language of the Fourth Gospel has recently been presented in a fine article by Schuyler Brown.[1] It would be superfluous to repeat it at length, but two features of his article are especially worthy of attention.

1. Characteristic of the article are the care and clarity with which the questions at issue are defined. In large measure the definitions are taken from the famous book of C. F. Burney, *The Aramaic Origin of the Fourth Gospel* (Oxford 1922). For example: an Aramaism is a grammatical or syntactical construction which, although unusual in Greek, is normal in Aramaic; a Hebraism is a construction that is normal in Hebrew but unusual in Greek; a Semitism is a construction which, although unusual in Greek, is normal in Aramaic and Hebrew. So much is self-evident but fundamental. Equally important is the distinction between *actual* and *virtual* translation. *Actual* translation needs no definition; *virtual* translation occurs when an author, although composing freely, introduces Semitic constructions because he naturally thinks in Semitic forms of expression. If the question of an Aramaic origin of the Fourth Gospel is under discussion, mistranslations are, accordingly, especially important. Brown, however, cites from the cautious and well-grounded work of M. Black[2] conditions whose strict application has the result that mistranslation becomes a tool that can be used only with great difficulty: the Greek in question must be so difficult that one can scarcely explain it otherwise; the false translation must be credible, i.e. one must be able to see how the translator could have derived it from the alleged Aramaic; finally, the alleged Aramaic must be unobjectionable. It does not follow from these strict conditions that no alleged mistranslations can be credible; they do, however, exclude many unnecessary and unscientific proposals. Black himself prefers to work with the concept of reinterpretation: the translator has not misunderstood his text and therefore mistranslated it, rather he has, spontaneously and in order to give a new interpretation, chosen a translation which, although possible, is not the most natural.

2. Brown shows that the scope of debate has narrowed somewhat in the course of two generations. Agreement has not been attained; perhaps it will never be. But the diversity of opinions is not so overwhelming as it was earlier.

> Few, if any, today are willing to go along with the notion of a complete Aramaic gospel, of which our present Fourth Gospel would be nothing but a slavish and inelegant translation. Few, on the other hand, are prepared to reject out of hand all Aramaic influence, or even the possibility that the author of the Fourth Gospel has made use of Aramaic sources. Yet the tension between the Hellenistic and Aramaic schools continues, and there are still plenty of doubtful cases which the former school will want to explain by analogy with other *Koine* documents, while the latter will tend to explain them by an appeal to an Aramaic original.[3]

Further, Brown considers the reaction to the discovery of the Qumran Aramaic. Here he is rightly cautious. We may, however, note in passing a particular linguistic form of the question which I have already raised. The right question is not whether the gospel is Hellenistic or Jewish. The question is rather where exactly we are able to locate the Jewish element which is present alongside the Hellenistic and how the Semitic element is combined with the Hellenistic or Gnostic. This question can be considered linguistically as well as theologically.

It should be clear that the limitations of this lecture do not permit a thorough linguistic investigation of the gospel. On the other hand it would be equally unsatisfactory to make only a few general observations at second hand. An independent investigation, even if of limited scope, is therefore required. If I may be permitted, I shall from the linguistic standpoint once again examine the prologue. It has often been said that the prologue is a translation of an Aramaic document or, more cautiously, that it is based upon Aramaic sources. Yet the judgement of scholars is not unanimous, and it is noteworthy that J. Jeremias, for example, who does not underestimate the Jewish element in the prologue, says that it was 'almost certainly composed in Greek'.[4]

The first step, too often neglected, should be simply to read through the prologue as a piece of Greek prose. Which parts or features would appear unusual or linguistically offensive to a Greek reader? From this standpoint the most striking feature of the prologue, as I see it, is its extraordinary simplicity. The reader who comes to the prologue from, for example, Plato—himself not the most complicated of Greek authors—cannot miss the almost naive mode of speech. I count, for example, thirty-two main verbs in independent clauses. In a comparable section at the outset of Plato's *Apology*—and this is perhaps the simplest of his dialogues— there are only seventeen, that is, approximately one-half as many. The remainder of this section of the *Apology* consists of various kinds of dependent clauses, while there are in the Johannine prologue five relative clauses, some subordinated participles, three ἵνα-clauses, three ὅτι-clauses, and a dependent infinitive—a very slim list. That the syntactical structure of Semitic languages is simpler than that of Greek is well known. Have we already then a pointer to the Semitic background and origin of the prologue? In my view the answer is no. For, although Greek is capable of the finest distinctions and the greatest complexity, there are also examples of very simple Greek. Such examples are found in personal letters of the papyri, which are not relevant here, except to remind us that not every Greek was a Thucydides, a fact which is often forgotten. More important instances are those that appear occasionally in Greek texts written for ceremonial, hieratic, or religious purposes. Still more relevant is the Greek of the magical and religious papyri, temple inscriptions praising the deeds of the gods, and certain parts of the Hermetic literature.[5]

The second step consists in reading the prologue afresh and on that basis asking which clauses and modes of speech seem strange or incorrect. These are not so numerous as one might at first suppose, for some expressions which at first appear un-Greek may be defended or explained as Greek. The following list of constructions, which on first glance do not seem to be Greek, is not complete, but it will suffice for our purpose.

v. 1. πρὸς τὸν θεόν   One would expect παρὰ τῷ θεῷ or, as elsewhere in the Gospel,[6] παρὰ τῷ πατρί. F. C. Burkitt suggested[7] that the meaning was 'the word was spoken to God'. Actually, however, this usage is too common in the New Testament to require a special explanation.[8] In the Hellenistic period the prepositions had lost their exactitude of meaning, a fact of which there is a second instance later in the prologue (εἰς, v. 18).

v. 3. ὃ γέγονεν   It would be more common to write ὧν γέγονεν 'not one of the things that have come into being'. At this point two things must be said: (*a*) the construction which we find is defensible—it is emphatic: not one thing which is has come to be without the word; (*b*) it is possible that the clauses should be divided differently, i.e., between οὐδὲ ἕν and ὃ γέγονεν.[9]

v. 6. ὄνομα αὐτῷ Ἰωάννης   Like the ἐγένετο ἄνθρωπος at the beginning of the verse this construction has Semitic parallels (for example, in the Old Testament).[10] Yet there are also Greek parallels, which Bernard[11] and Colwell[12] cite.

v. 7. εἰς μαρτυρίαν   This expression is also Greek; according to Liddell–Scott[13] εἰς can be used 'of purpose or object'; it is not clear to me why Bultmann (ad loc.) is unwilling to recognize Plato, *Leges* xi. 937a (ὁ δ' εἰς μαρτυρίαν κληθείς) as a parallel.

v. 8. The elliptical use of ἀλλ' ἵνα is a Johannine form of speech,[14] but not un-Greek.

v. 9.　Periphrastic tenses are not unknown in Greek; according to Lagrange (ad loc.), however, the separation of the
participle from the imperfect of εἶναι is surprising; compare,
however, 2.6; 10.40; 18.30. Early patristic interpretation
suggests that a Greek would perhaps find it natural to read
the sentence in a different way, that is, he would take the
ἐρχόμενον not with φῶς ἦν, but with πάντα ἄνθρωπον, which
is admittedly possible.[15]

v. 12.　The verse begins with a characteristic *casus pendens*.
Black,[16] however, is correct in saying that this construction
'is not specially a Semitism. It is used with effect in classical
Greek, and parallels to instances in the Gospels have been
cited from the papyri and elsewhere.' Black, like Burney,[17]
observes the relative frequency of the *casus pendens* in the
Gospel of John, especially in words which are ascribed to
Jesus and which could have originated in Aramaic tradition.
In the prologue, however, there is no word of Jesus; we must
therefore recognize a Johannine stylistic characteristic which
is not un-Greek.

In the same verse the dependence of the infinite (γενέσθαι)
on the noun (ἐξουσίαν) does not seem to be idiomatic.　But
(*a*) John uses ἐξουσίαν ἔχειν and similar expressions for 'to
be able'[18] and (*b*) there are Greek parallels, for example, in
the *Corpus Hermeticum* 1.28: ἔχοντες ἐξουσίαν τῆς ἀθανασίας
μεταλαβεῖν.

v. 13.　The use of the plural αἵματα is a point of debate.
Turner[19] speaks of it as a classical plural. The question may
perhaps be passed over, however.

v. 14.　To a Greek the clause σὰρξ ἐγένετο would sound
strange. Probably he would be uncertain whether it meant
birth, entry on the public scene (as in v. 6), transformation,
or something else. That, however, would be the consequence
of the strangeness of the thought which John attempts to
express and not of the unclarity of the expression.

The indeclinable use of πλήρης, although generally post-classical, would give a Hellenistic reader no trouble.[20]

v. 15. The perfect κέκραγεν is at first glance surprising. But this verb stands 'frequently in the perfect with present sense'.[21] Moulton[22] supports this idiomatic usage with the help of the LXX; but that leads perhaps to the conclusion that it was biblical Greek[23] which preserved the classical use of the perfect.[24]

In the same verse the comparative use of πρῶτος is not to be defended; but at this time πρότερος was certainly on the decline.

v. 16 I do not believe that a Greek would have found χάριν ἀντὶ χάριτος simple. The difficulty, however, lies in the brevity of the expression. The meaning is suggested by the often quoted passage in Philo, *De Post. Caini* 145.[25] New grace is given instead of old, so that one is always dependent on nothing other than grace.

v. 17. νόμον διδόναι is not a common Greek expression; νόμον τιθέναι or τίθεσθαι is usually found. That which is non-Greek, however, lies rather in the meaning of the noun than in the verb. If νόμος is the law of a Greek city, τιθέναι is the correct corresponding verb. But in the Johannine context νόμος = תורה; and that is a completely different concept which naturally requires another verb. The Torah was not simply a law-book, but God's gracious self-communication.[26] It has the character of a gift, so that διδόναι would be the correct word.

v. 18. In εἰς τὸν κόλπον (cf. the use of πρός in v. 1) the preposition is 'incorrectly' used: one expects ἐν with the dative. But the interchange of εἰς and ἐν was not unusual in the Hellenistic period;[27] only an Atticistic reader would take offence at it.

This sketch suggests the view that a Greek reader would not have been disturbed very much by the linguistic and syntactical character of the prologue. Some of the alleged Semitisms of the prologue have already been discussed; but we must now ask which if any of them are actually convincing. The following examples are taken from the works of Burney,[28] Black,[29] Beyer,[30] and others. I choose only such alleged Semitisms as have a claim to be taken seriously.

It is possible that the Aramaic לות contributed to the free use of πρός in v. 1, but since the usage is widespread,[31] no conclusions can be drawn concerning John and his sources. Neither actual nor virtual translation is suggested.

The argument that ἐν αὐτῷ (v. 4) is a mistranslation of ביה, which should be translated as δι᾽ αὐτοῦ (as in v. 3), is not convincing, as Bultmann (ad loc.) has already shown; that another preposition is used is rather an argument for beginning a new sentence with the words ἐν αὐτῷ. Creation was *through* the word, but life was *in* him. In v. 5 it would be methodologically incorrect to call in question the tense of φαίνει and to ascribe it to the misunderstanding of an Aramaic original. That would be possible only if the Greek present tense had to be labelled intolerable. But the present is not impossible, so that there is no need to conjecture a false translation.

We have already seen that ἐγένετο ἄνθρωπος, ὄνομα αὐτῷ Ἰωάννης is not un-Greek. Yet the sentence sounds like the Old Testament. That is no indication of an Aramaic original, however. Rather, it recalls the Hebrew of the Old Testament. That yields an important observation. If John departs from the metaphysics of the first verses in order to describe an historical person, he does so in the language of the Old Testament. This does not suggest Greek interpolation into a Semitic Logos-hymn.

In v. 8 Turner[32] sees, but with reservations, an example of the imperatival use of ἵνα and thinks that this usage was originally Semitic. It is very doubtful, however, whether imperatival ἵνα is Semitic and equally doubtful whether ἵνα in v. 8 is imperatival.

In vv. 10 and 11 Beyer[33] sees a possible Semitism in the conditional parataxis of 'He was in the world, yet . . .; he came to his own, yet . . .'. This is very doubtful. Actually these verses contain a Greek form of speech, which cannot be Aramaic. The Greek distinguishes between τὰ ἴδια, to which the Word came, and οἱ ἴδιοι, who were unwilling to receive it. Such a distinction would be difficult to carry through in Aramaic; for both τὰ ἴδια and οἱ ἴδιοι, one would write דילה.[34]

Beyer[35] also finds a Semitism in v. 12. Here again it is difficult to follow him. ὅσοι δὲ ἔλαβον *could* be a pluralized Greek equivalent of the Aramaic singular (. . . כל ד); but that may not be considered proof of a Semitism. Had the Greek been παντὶ δὲ λαβόντι, that would perhaps constitute grounds for the argument, but this is exactly what does not stand in the text. The plural is Greek and could have been Greek from the beginning.

The ἐξουσίαν διδόναι γενέσθαι of the same verse has already been discussed.[36] There are no grounds for supposing that it is a translation or a further development of the Semitic נתן להם וילהת.

The striking result of our investigation is that no one of the alleged Semitisms of the prologue is truly convincing. There is no syntactical support for the view that the evangelist drew upon Aramaic sources in the prologue. Probably he himself wrote the entire piece—a conclusion which must influence interpretation. In the prologue, however, (*a*) the vocabulary and (*b*) the alleged poetic form remain to be investigated.

(*a*) *Vocabulary*   G. D. Kilpatrick[37] has attempted to prove that the Johannine vocabulary (and therefore Johannine thought) is essentially that of Hellenistic Judaism and has no

special connection with the *Corpus Hermeticum*.³⁸ Conse-
quently the Hermetica may be excluded from the discussion
of the interpretation of the gospel. We are able to test his
assertion with respect to the prologue.

First, we assemble a list of important words, excluding
pronouns, prepositions, and the like, which do not contribute to the discussion. The following list will suffice: ἀλήθεια,
ἀληθινός, ἀποστέλλειν, ἀρχή, γεννᾶν, δόξα, ἐξηγεῖσθαι, ἐξουσία,
ζωή, θεᾶσθαι, καταλαμβάνειν, κόλπος, κόσμος, λόγος, μαρτυρεῖν,
μαρτυρία, μονογενής, νόμος, ὁρᾶν, παραλαμβάνειν, πιστεύειν,
πλήρωμα, σάρξ, σκηνοῦν, σκοτία, τέκνον, φαίνειν, φῶς, φωτίζειν,
χάρις (30). All these words occur in the LXX; it would be
hasty, however, to conclude from this fact that the speech of
the prologue corresponds exactly to that of the LXX. The
LXX is a large book with a rich vocabulary, and most of the
words cited above are so common as to be of little worth for
statistical purposes. They are common to the LXX, but they
are also present in almost every sphere of Greek literature.
Such words are ἀλήθεια (more must be said later about this
word), ἀληθινός (I shall also come back to this word),
ἀποστέλλειν, ἀρχή (yet it is certain that John 1.1 plays on
Gen. 1.1), γεννᾶν (I shall also return to this word), δόξα,
ζωή, καταλαμβάνειν, κόλπος, λόγος (here the question of the
origin of John's usage remains open), νόμος, ὁρᾶν, παραλαμβάνειν, πιστεύειν, σάρξ, τέκνον (the usage in the prologue leads
to a question which I must consider later), φαίνειν, φῶς,
φωτίζειν, χάρις (I shall later consider the use of this word in
connection with ἀλήθεια). These are twenty words, two-
thirds of the total. The remaining ten words may be re-
viewed briefly. σκοτία appears only three times in the LXX.
σκότος is much more frequent. This difference reflects
general Greek usage. It follows that nothing can be based
on the choice of σκοτία, though it must be conceded that
John has taken no trouble to choose the LXX-form. Precisely the same observation may be made in view of John's

use of μαρτυρεῖν and μαρτυρία. These forms are much less frequent in the LXX than the neuter μαρτύριον. κόσμος and ἐξουσία occur fairly frequently in the LXX, but they are much more common in the books written originally in Greek than in those translated out of Hebrew.[39] σκηνοῦν is infrequent in the LXX (five times); the same is true of θεᾶσθαι;[40] on the other hand, σκηνοῦν and θεᾶσθαι appear frequently outside the LXX. μονογενής is rare in the LXX, but the word is infrequent in Greek generally; the Johannine use of it is surely not to be derived from the Old Testament. πλήρωμα, not an uncommon word in Greek, plays no great role in the LXX (fourteen times; eleven times of the content of the earth and sea). ἐξηγεῖσθαι, which is found nine times in the LXX, is attested in connection with divine revelation only in Job 12.8; 28.7; in non-biblical Greek it occurs more frequently in a religious sense.

This group of words suggests that a non-biblical influence has affected Johannine language. If it can be said that John shares this influence with the author of the Wisdom of Solomon,[41] and perhaps with Philo,[42] then it must also be conceded that as an author he wrote for a Greek, non-Jewish audience.

But the words which are frequent in the LXX may also be of significance. For example, γεννᾶν and τέκνον are found frequently in the LXX as well as in Greek generally. John, however, uses them of the τέκνα θεοῦ, who ἐκ θεοῦ ἐγεννήθησαν. This is certainly not the usage of the LXX. Even passages such as Deut. 32.18 and Ps. 2.7 do not mean what John meant when he speaks of those who through faith are reborn to a new existence (cf. 3.3,5). The speech is ordinary Greek; the thought is not that of the Old Testament. With somewhat more reservation, the same may be said of ἀληθινός. The exact meaning of the term in Johannine usage is debated; but even if the word signifies much less than the Platonic *ideal*, it goes far beyond the concept of speaking the truth. Finally, we observe the use of χάρις καὶ ἀλήθεια. As every commentator points out, the Greek expression corresponds to the Hebrew חסד ואמת. But by χάρις καὶ ἀλήθεια John does not intend what the Old Testament means by חסד ואמת. In the Old Testament that expression means 'lasting solidarity'.[43] Outside the prologue the word χάρις does not appear in the Fourth Gospel; ἀλήθεια, however, suggests the concept of reality.

The non-biblical, non-Jewish background of Johannine language should now be more closely defined, but that cannot be done for two reasons: time does not permit it, and it would not be appropriate in a lecture on Judaism. It suffices to observe (i) that John uses a simple and limited vocabulary of average Greek, which also appears in the LXX; (ii) that he often, but not always, chooses words which are characteristic of the LXX; (iii) that he uses Old Testament words with a new meaning. On the basis of his language as well as from other perspectives one must judge that Judaism appears as only one element and, indeed, as one element in close connection with others, in the Fourth Gospel.

(*b*) *Literary Form*   There remains the question of the original form of the prologue. It is often maintained that the prologue was composed originally as verse. The repeated and various efforts at reconstruction, however, increasingly raise suspicions about the ability of scholars to reconstruct a prologue or *Urprolog* that will seem convincing as a piece of Aramaic poetry.

The most recent commentator, R. E. Brown,[44] arranges the prologue in the following manner:

FIRST STROPHE

1   In the beginning was the Word;
    the Word was in God's presence,
    and the Word was God.
2   He was present with God in the beginning.

SECOND STROPHE

3 Through him all things came into being,
     and apart from him not a thing came to be.
4 That which had come to be in him was life,
     and this life was the light of men.
5 The light shines on in the darkness,
     for the darkness did not overcome it.

(6 There was sent by God a man named John   7 who came as a witness to testify to the light so that through him all men might believe— 8 but only to testify to the light, for he himself was not the light. 9 The real light which gives light to every man was coming into the world!)

THIRD STROPHE

10 He was in the world,
      and the world was made by him;
      yet the world did not recognize him.
11 To his own he came;
      yet his own people did not accept him.
12 But all those who did accept him
      he empowered to become God's children.

That is, those who believe in his name—13 those who were begotten, not by blood, nor by carnal desire, nor by man's desire, but by God.

FOURTH STROPHE

14 And the Word became flesh
      and made his dwelling among us.
      And we have seen his glory,
      the glory of an only Son coming from the Father,
      filled with enduring love.

(15 John testified to him by proclaiming: 'This is he of whom I said, "The one who comes after me ranks ahead of me, for he existed before me." ')

16 And of his fullness
      we have all had a share—
      love in place of love.

17 For while the Law was a gift through Moses, this enduring love came through Jesus Christ. 18 No one has ever seen God; it is God the only Son, ever at the Father's side, who has revealed Him.

This presentation is no more convincing than earlier attempts to attain the same goal. The strophes are irregular. The first contains two couplets, the second three. The third begins with an uneven triplet and continues with two couplets. The fourth contains first a group with five lines and then a group with three. If the principal distinguishing mark of the verse is *parallelismus membrorum*, one asks why verses 17 and 18 are not included, but are printed as prose. The parallelism is better in these verses than in some others. They could be arranged as follows:

> For while the Law was a gift through Moses,
> Enduring love came through Jesus Christ.
> No one has ever seen God;
> It is the only Son [ever at the Father's side] who
>   has revealed him.

One may compare v. 12, in which there is no parallelism:

> But all those who did accept him
> he empowered to become God's children.

That this latter verse is a prose sentence becomes even clearer if the words 'who believe in his name' are not excised. But Brown presents the verse as if it were a couplet of parallel lines.

One can scarcely avoid the conclusion that Brown's analysis, which does not differ essentially from the others, stands on no sure footing. Between the different parts of the prologue there is only one objective difference: the majority deal with the person of Jesus, who is presented as the pre-existent, Incarnate Word, while others sketch the subordinated form of John, who bears witness to his own role as forerunner.

This observation leads to a further question, which cannot be dealt with in this treatment of the prologue. It concerns both its content and form. Are the references to John the Baptist an original part of the prologue, or are they redactional insertions in a previously existing work, one which was already complete? I can find no reason for modifying the answer to this question which I have already given,[45] but I should like to take it a little further.

There are not many literary products which, like Melchizedek, are without ancestry. So it is possible, or indeed probable, that the evangelist had read and thought about Genesis, the Wisdom of Solomon, the first verses of the Gospel of Mark, and the first chapter of the Gospel of Luke. One must also reckon with other sources which we are not able to identify so exactly: Gnostic hymns such as the Odes of Solomon and rabbinic thinking concerning the Torah. That the evangelist was acquainted with such sources and felt free to incorporate words or sentences from them into his own work is quite probable. For their part Mark and Luke had already mentioned the Baptist in the first lines of their gospels. Conceivably, John likewise, although he also used non-Christian sources, wrote in the prologue an introduction for a gospel, namely, that gospel which he was about to write, or perhaps had already written. It could be that the evangelist himself was involved in dispute with disciples of John the Baptist.[46] In any case, the earlier tradition emphasized that John the Baptist was a necessary element of the background and the beginning of the gospel history. The evangelist was about to handle this element historically, and thus to give an account (1.19–37) of the answer of the Baptist to the official Jewish questioning, his witness about Jesus, and the departure of his disciples to follow Jesus. It is precisely these stories that he summarizes in the prologue in theological terms, just as he summarizes there the theological significance of the historical Jesus—the one the light, the other the witness to that light.

This long discussion is not without its consequences for the general question of the relation of the gospel to Judaism. If the question is put simply—Jewish or Greek?—no simple answer is possible. It cannot be proved that the prologue has been translated out of Aramaic; it is not even possible to demonstrate virtual translation. Yet the almost complete identity of the vocabulary with the LXX is surely not coincidental. Nevertheless, the language of the prologue shows a certain independence of the LXX, and occasionally a diversity of thought is disguised by a superficial identity of vocabulary. The prologue is not poetry, although an occasional structural parallelism occurs. It is rather a rhythmic, hieratic prose, suitable for the presentation of religious mysteries. It reminds one of other theological and cultic literature of a similar sort.[47] Yet the prologue is punctuated with statements about that very earthy figure, John the Baptist. This last observation affords us a necessary key: the prologue is a theological evaluation of the historical life of Jesus, and nothing discloses this fact so clearly as the related fact that it at the same time presents a theological evaluation of the historical life of the Baptist. This, however, leads to the important conclusion that the prologue is nothing other than a Christian work, and that means, further, that the Jewish and Gnostic material which one can discover in the prologue has already been thought through in the mind of the author. He did not invent the mutual interpenetration of Judaism and Gnosis; it already existed, and he chose it as the means of expressing Christian truth.[48] In this process he also contributed to the interpenetration of both spheres.

From this discussion of the language and content of the prologue I turn to a broader question: What relation have the new discoveries in Palestinian archaeology and topography to the origin and interpretation of the gospel? In recent years several scholars have maintained that these discoveries have confirmed the historical accuracy and at the same time the Jewish—indeed the Palestinian—origin of the gospel. How do matters actually stand?

I agree with Lagrange's demand, seconded by R. D. Potter,[49] for a 'realist attitude' to the gospel. In my opinion John very seldom uses geographical details to express theological points. He repeats those details because he has found them in the tradition. Exegetes, however, who are neither archaeologists nor experts in Palestinian topography should here exert a restraining influence. It seems that there are some problems to which we are now at last finding the answers; one thinks, for example, of the book of J. Jeremias, *The Rediscovery of Bethesda* (Louisville 1966).[50] The location of the pool is no longer uncertain, even if the name— Bethesda, Bethzatha, Bethsaida—is still somewhat doubtful. There are, however, some other questions concerning which the non-archaeologist feels he must wait somewhat longer before he can enjoy full certainty. I shall go through the instances adduced by Potter with a sceptical eye.

John 4 offers the first example. While Potter identifies Sychar with the modern Askar, Albright[51] rejects this identification; with the Old Syriac he reads Sychem instead of Sychar, and locates the incident in Balatah. The exegete does well to leave this question for his colleagues to settle; perhaps agreement will eventually be reached. In the meantime, however, he will be within his rights if he questions the realism of the explanation of 4.35 which Potter maintains: 'Further we can, at the right season, see from Jacob's Well τὰς χώρας ὅτι λευκαί εἰσιν as we glance over the great level plain stretching south and east. No passage could show better that our author knew this bit of Samaria well.'[52] Perhaps the evangelist (or the author of a source) actually knew this landscape well; one cannot deny the possibility. But that he was not thinking of a harvest in the southern Palestinian plains the following words show clearly: ἤδη ὁ θερίζων μισθὸν λαμβάνει καὶ συνάγει καρπὸν εἰς ζωὴν αἰώνιον. 'Fruit for eternal life' was not a harvest to be gathered in the grain fields of Samaria.

There follow two instances which can be quickly disposed of. There are today few scholars who would defend the reading Bethabara (1.28), the conjecture of Origen. Also, it is surely correct that the most probable location of Cana is situated on higher ground than Capernaum, so that the Johannine καταβαίνειν (2.12) is apposite.

Differences of opinion among the experts put the identification of Salim in doubt. Potter places this locality south of Beisan,[53] and agrees with Lagrange in concluding: 'In any case the evangelist here gives proof of his precise knowledge of these places.' Albright,[54] on the other hand, prefers the modern Salim, southeast of Nablus and Shechem. Here also the exegete is able to make no decision; yet he may suspect that one—or perhaps both—of the experts is somewhat too confident.

With respect to Jerusalem, Potter believes that 'There is no reason for doubting that this [Solomon's porch] was the colonnaded portico which lined the eastern wall of the present day Haram area.'[55] But there are also no compelling grounds for believing this. Many years ago Lake[56] summarized all that can be said with certainty: 'The Porch of Solomon is more likely to have been on the east than anywhere else, though the usual statement that it certainly was there is unwarranted.'

Still more important is the debate over the identification of the pavement (τὸ λιθόστρωτον) called Gabbatha (19.13). According to L. H. Vincent[57] this was to be sought in the court of the fortress Antonia, in which, in his opinion, Pilate had his headquarters at the time of the Passover when Jesus

was crucified. P. Benoit,[58] however, thinks that the prae-
torium was located in the castle of Herod on the western
hill. Of course, it cannot be proved that there was a λιθόστρωτον in this castle; but, as Potter agrees, it is in no way
impossible, quite probable, rather, that the castle contained
a paved floor. Albright, who noted the difference of opinion
between Vincent and Benoit, writes:[59] 'It may be emphasized that Benoit's view would not appreciably affect our
contention here'—the contention, that is, that topographical
observations could prove that John possessed a good old
tradition which the synoptic evangelists did not know. But
in fact this contention is in no sense well-founded, except in
the sense which would not satisfy Albright, namely, that the
evangelist retained topographical names whose significance
he no longer understood.

If one investigates the gospel from the standpoint of
literary and historical criticism, it is scarcely to be doubted
that the archaeological material requires a more cautious
treatment than some of the most skilful specialists have been
prepared to give it. The archaeologists, however, are in no
position to dictate to the exegetes. We may be confident
that if John used place names he meant to refer to places
and not to allegorical mysteries. It is most improbable that
he invented place names or tied them to events in a purely
arbitrary way. Names and events were already bound together when they reached the evangelist. Such a state of
affairs suggests a Palestinian origin, at least for the narrative
material. That is not surprising. The reconstruction of a
topography, or of a biographical itinerary, is so difficult,
however, that one may doubt whether the evangelist, the
last editor of the gospel in its present form, was interested
in topography at all.[60] Topographical precision could neither
prove nor refute what he wished to say by means of his
gospel.[61]

I summarize in very brief compass: A Jewish element in

the Fourth Gospel cannot be denied. The language recalls the Old Testament; the narratives, far from being allegorical inventions, are tied to topographical details.[62] This Jewish element is, however, too weak to permit the conclusion that John wrote only for a Jewish audience or that his main intention was to transmit with precision a Palestinian tradition. Our question, therefore, remains open. The relation of John to Judaism is still to be defined.

3

Judaism in
the Johannine Period

In these four lectures, which have not set as their goal a general survey of the Fourth Gospel, but rather a definition of its relations to Judaism, it is obviously impossible to discuss thoroughly the date at which the gospel was written. To do so would mean that I should have to discuss many circumstances within and without the gospel which I do not have time to mention. But because the date of composition is important for our purpose, I may be permitted the general observation that the traditional opinion, which also receives support from modern criticism, still seems to be tenable. According to this view the gospel was written near the end of the first century.[1]

Now it is clear that the consideration of the relation of this gospel to Judaism is a very involved problem, and the later the gospel is dated the more involved the problem becomes. The gospel as a whole seems intended to be a report about the life and teaching of Jesus. But is that really its intention? Further very difficult problems arise as soon as one asks how far any single part of the gospel is an accurate and truly historically trustworthy report, and whether the evangelist wanted to provide such a report at all. Now it is important and incontrovertible that the gospel arose only because Jesus was what he was and spoke and acted as he did. At least in this sense the gospel is based upon the life and teaching of Jesus. This life was lived and this teaching delivered within

Judaism—Palestinian Judaism in the period of the governor Pontius Pilate and Herod the Tetrarch. In this fact must be recognized one element, even if not a very important one, among the gospel's relations with Judaism.

After the death and resurrection of Jesus the connection between the earliest Christian community, whose history we can glimpse in the New Testament, and Judaism, whose development up to the time of the uprising against Rome Josephus enables us to trace, continued. During this period Christianity and Judaism were in contact with each other; however, in time each took a changed form. As a whole Christianity became a non-Jewish organization. Judaism presents a very complex picture, but one can say that on the whole it became increasingly nationalistic. The war of 66–70 then separated the church from its roots in Palestine and transformed Israel from a national theocracy into a stateless church. Not that Israel ceased altogether to think of itself in national, political, and military terms; this kind of self-consciousness was still present and was to burst forth again in the Bar Cocheba rebellion. But Jewish nationalism had nevertheless received a severe blow, and in the seventies and eighties Judaism was re-established on a basis that was not primarily nationalistic. During this critical time both religions changed radically. But in this process they did remain in some contact with one another, and one may assume that this contact is reflected in the gospel tradition. The investigation of the Synoptic Gospels shows that tensions between Jews and Christians did, in fact, influence the tradition.[2] So we must reckon with the possibility that the traditional material used in the Fourth Gospel did not remain untouched by this development, since the latest stages of the interaction, which had begun with the life and teaching of Jesus, occurred in the eighties and nineties, that is, in the time of the reconstitution of Judaism following the debacle of the year 70.

In the light of such considerations it is hardly satisfactory to say that the gospel refers to Jewish feasts; that it recalls Jewish exegesis of the Old Testament; that it utilizes Jewish arguments; and that therefore it is essentially and fundamentally a Jewish book. Apart from the fact that the gospel also manifests non-Jewish characteristics, we must ask with what Judaism the gospel was in contact and in what relation to this Judaism it stood.

We ask, therefore, in this third lecture: What do we know of Judaism and of the interreaction of the two religions, Judaism and Christianity, at the end of the first century?[3]

I begin with a negative observation which so far as I know has been somewhat overlooked. Anyone who is familiar with the Jewish literature of the last two centuries before Christ would have expected the fall of Jerusalem in the year 70 to have been the occasion of an outbreak of apocalyptic. As Antiochus' profanation of the temple called forth the Book of Daniel and the less provocative act of Pompey the Psalms of Solomon, so one would have expected the epoch-making assault of Titus to have awakened the apocalyptic hope for divine intervention and vengeance. Yet this seems not to have happened. Naturally, the apocalypses raise difficult questions not only about their time of composition, but also with respect to their unity. Nor is it at all clear which apocalypses are Jewish, which are Christian, and which are Jewish with pronounced Christian redaction. Fourth Ezra and perhaps also the Apocalypse of Baruch were published during this period. Yet there is scarcely any essentially Jewish apocalyptic material which clearly mirrors the events of the year 70—the one exception being the Apocalypse of Abraham. Here too many details are unclear, but the references in the Apocalypse of Abraham 27 can scarcely be misunderstood:[4]

> And I looked and saw: lo! the picture swayed and [from it] emerged, on its left side, a heathen people, and they pillaged

those who were on the right side, men and women and children:
[some they slaughtered,] others they retained with themselves.
Lo! I saw them run towards them through four entrances, and
they burnt the Temple with fire, and the holy things that were
therein they plundered.

And I said: 'O Eternal One! Lo! the people (that spring)
from me, whom Thou hast accepted, the hordes of the heathen
do plunder, and some they kill, while others they hold fast as
aliens, and the Temple they have burnt with fire, and the
beautiful things therein they do rob [and destroy]. O Eternal,
Mighty One! If this be so, wherefore hast Thou now lacerated
my heart, and why should this be so?'

The answer to this question is that the temple was destroyed on account of Israel's sin. Abraham asks how long
the destruction and suffering are to last. The answer is hid-
den in mysterious apocalyptic writing of the usual kind, but
its essential meaning is that the time of deliverance, of the
End, is near.

Apart from this apocalypse there is little Jewish apocalyptic material that arose during this period, even though one
can discern an abundance of Christian apocalyptic currents,
notably the apocalypses in the Synoptic Gospels and the
Apocalypse of John. Although a re-emergence of Jewish
apocalyptic in this period might have been expected, this
was actually the time of its disappearance. It might be added
that during this period Christians took over Jewish apocalypses and interpolated them. For the most part, however, it
was a time when Jews and Christians went their separate
ways as far as apocalyptic was concerned.

It may also be observed—and the observation is not unimportant—that there are traces of Gnosis in the Apocalypse
of Abraham. One example is the use of 'left' and 'right' in
the passage that I cited. G. H. Box[5] writes: 'The use of
"right" and "left" throughout these chapters is notable.
The conception of the right side being the source of light and

purity, while the left is the source of darkness and impurity, is Gnostic, and passed from the Gnostics into the Kabbalah.' Box distinguishes between such Gnostic traces and interpolations introduced by Christian Gnostics and maintains: 'The phenomena suggest that the Book is an essentially Jewish one, which may have been used and read by Gnostic Christians, and adapted by slight revision to make it acceptable to such readers.'[6]

One may say with some probability that the apocalyptic movement within Judaism lost its strength in the second half of the first century. It is noteworthy that in the process of formulating the Old Testament canon in Jamnia only one apocalyptic book was accepted.[7] Among Christians, however, the apocalyptic movement received a powerful impulse. The preaching of Jesus, followed by his death and resurrection, had awakened a lively hope that the kingdom of God would come very soon. The earliest form of this hope was dissipated with the disappearance of the first Christian generation;[8] but just at this time the hope was renewed by the fall of Jerusalem and the destruction of the temple. There existed a tradition, according to which Jesus prophesied the destruction of the temple.[9] If this prediction had been fulfilled, then could the fulfilment of the others, the predictions of the end of the present age and the inbreaking of the coming age, be far behind?

In such ways many Christians reacted to the shattering military and political events. This reaction is understandable, and in some measure it confirmed and reanimated the early Christian apocalyptic tradition. The Fourth Evangelist did not, however, share in this reaction. It is incorrect to maintain that the Fourth Gospel contains no futuristic eschatology;[10] it is only correct to say that apocalyptic is not characteristic of the gospel. John saw that the new situation in which Judaism and Christianity found themselves required not the staunch maintenance of the expectation of a sudden turn of fortune, but an earnest attempt to think through theological problems. He, like some Jews,[11] could see that the meaning of his period lay not in an imminent end that was to be proclaimed, but in the necessity of preparation for an unexpected and uncertain future. With these preliminary observations[12] I do not mean to imply that John affirmed and imitated the non-apocalyptic Jewish reaction. That would have been highly unlikely. One notes, however, a similarity between John and the Judaism of his time on the one hand, and, on the other, a dissimilarity between John and contemporary Christianity.

A further comparison makes this similarity clearer. It is well known that in this period the famous Johanan ben Zakkai was the architect of a restored Judaism. According to F. C. Burkitt[13] Johanan consciously opposed apocalyptic. He cites Ber. R. 44, 25:

> On that day the Lord bound himself with respect to Abraham by the following stipulation (Gen. 15.18). R. Judah . . . said: R. Johanan b. Zakkai . . . and R. Aqiba . . . The one said: God revealed this world to Abraham but he did not reveal the world to come. . . . The other said: He revealed to him both this world and the world to come.[14]

If, according to one of the rabbis, the secrets of the world to come were not revealed to Abraham, they would *a fortiori* not be revealed to anyone else. J. Neusner[15] noted that the passage would have been more helpful to Burkitt if it had made clear 'which of the two Rabbis held which opinion'. Yet there is no great difficulty. Precisely the content of the account of the life and teaching of Johanan which Neusner himself has written, not to mention what we already know of Aqiba, makes the narrative clear. When he hailed Bar Cocheba as Messiah, Aqiba voiced his conviction that an apocalyptic future lay ahead, while Johanan, as Neusner shows, concentrated on dealing with the present and so laying a firm foundation for his people. These facts are sufficient to make the meaning clear.[16]

In order to prove his assertion[17] that 'Johanan [was] always skeptical of messianic movements among the people' Neusner cites Aboth d. R. Nathan 31:

> If you have a sapling in your hand and it is said to you, 'Behold, There is the Messiah,'—go on with your planting, and afterward go out ond receive him.[18]

Thus Johanan expected no quick solution, although he believed that repentance would bring redemption. Neusner writes:[19]

> [His program] was, first, to provide the people with a source of genuine comfort by showing them how they might extricate themselves from the consequences of their sins. Second, he placed new emphasis upon those means of serving the Creator which had survived the devastated sanctuary. Finally, he offered a comprehensive program for the religious life, a program capable of meeting this and any future vicissitude in Israel's history. By concentrating on the immediate problems of the day, Johanan showed how to transcend history itself —not through eschatological vision, but through concrete actions in the workaday world.

He elevated to prominence the enduring elements in Judaism and came to understand the reward for obedience individualistically rather than nationalistically.[20] Accordingly (Midr. Qoh. 9, 8 [42a]) Johanan interpreted Eccles. 9.8 ('Let your garments be always white; let not oil be lacking on your head') as follows:

> If the scriptures speak of white clothes, how many white clothes have the nations of the world! And if the scriptures speak of good oils, how many good oils have the people of the world! But look, they speak rather only of fulfilling the commandments and of good works and of the study of the Torah.[21]

It is instructive to compare this interpretation with the famous words of Simeon the Just in Aboth 1.2. Simeon said that the world rests upon three things, upon the Torah, the temple service, and deeds of love. For the עבודה (the temple service) Johanan substitutes the fulfilling of the commandments. These could be performed by any individual Israelite —without the temple.[22]

The result of Johanan's activity in the restoration of Judaism was to express its thought about the future almost exclusively in individual form. Thus a realm had been created in which the Israelite could continue to serve God and could hope for his own resurrection and for eternal life. The importance of this observation for the investigation of the Fourth Gospel is not difficult to grasp.

We now recall a second characteristic of the Judaism of this period. At this time steps had been taken to settle the problem of Jewish Christians. One thinks, of course, of the *Birkath ha-minim*, usually cited in the commentaries in relation to 9.22 and 16.2;[23] but this benediction must be put in a broader context. Justin (*Trypho* 16) describes the Jews as καταρώμενοι ἐν ταῖς συναγωγαῖς ὑμῶν τοὺς πιστεύοντας ἐπὶ τὸν χριστόν. Later (*Trypho* 137) he says that this malediction followed μετὰ τὴν προσευχήν, after the prayer. Now Justin scarcely gives us a disinterested report of what went on in the synagogue. But his is not our only attestation of the hatred that existed between Jews and Christians. For example, the Martyrdom of Polycarp shows that Jews were particularly zealous in the persecution of the church of Smyrna.[24] Already in the middle of the second century there existed hatred between Jews and Gentile Christians. Between Jews and Jewish Christians it must have developed earlier.

The time of composition and original purpose of the ברכת המינים are disputed. In a summary sketch such as this I cannot hope to contribute anything new to the discussion. Therefore, I only set forth the most important facts. The clearest report on their origin is found in b. Berakhoth 28b:

> Rabban Gamaliel said to the Sages: Is there anyone among you who can compose a benediction relating to the Minim? Samuel the Less stood up and composed it.

We need not inquire further about the date of composition of the Benediction. Anything that occurred in the period of Gamaliel occurred in the period of the Fourth Gospel. A further question is whether the passage cited, in its original form, referred not only to the מינים, but also to the נוצרים. I need not go into this question, for the word מינים includes the Jewish Christians, even if they are not meant exclusively. נוצרים is perhaps to be understood as a retranslation of Ναζωραῖοι.[25] Whether this Benediction is a complete explanation of the Johannine ἀποσυνάγωγος[26] remains a further question. One may, however, scarcely doubt that it was used to expose heretical—and especially Christian—members of the synagogue.

A comparable alteration of the hitherto existing usage may be seen in the benediction that follows upon the Shema. This reads: ברוך שם כבוד מלכותו לעולם ועד. 'Blessed be the name of the glory of his kingdom for ever and ever.' In earlier times these words were uttered in a subdued voice. In Babylonia, where Christians constituted no problem, this practice was not altered. In the west, however, it was decided that the benediction should be spoken in a louder voice, doubtless in order to make it more difficult for Christians to introduce secret modifications into the proclamation of the unity of God.

At other points too one can recognize a conscious defence of the Jewish teaching on unity. For example, one reads in the Passover Haggada:

> The Lord led us out of Egypt with a mighty hand and an outstretched arm and with great terror, through signs and

wonders (Deut. 26.8). The Lord led us out of the land of
Egypt—not by an angel, not by a seraph, not by a messenger;
but the Holy One, blessed be he, in his own glory and by himself (בעצמו), as it is said: I will in the same night go through
the land of Egypt and slay all the firstborn in Egypt, both man
and beast, and I will manifest my judgement against all the
gods of the Egyptians: I, the Lord (אני יי: Exod. 12.12). *I
will in the same night go through Egypt*: I myself and not an angel
(אני ולא מלאך). *And I will slay the firstborn in Egypt*, I myself
and not a seraph (אני ולא שרף). *And I will manifest my judgement
against all the gods of Egypt*: I myself and not the messenger
(אני ולא השליח). *I, the Lord*: I am he and not another (אני הוא
ולא אחר).

Probably this repeated emphasis upon the sole activity of
God developed out of polemic against Christians.[27] Especially important is the expression השליח.[28] Only once in the
New Testament (Heb. 3.1) is Jesus called ὁ ἀπόστολος, but
in the Gospel of John the terms ἀποστέλλειν and πέμπειν
occur very frequently, and there is, moreover, no concept
which is more important to the evangelist than that which
designates Jesus as the one sent by the Father. This concept
is often—and correctly—defined as Gnostic. It is more
important, however, that it was known within Judaism and
that Christians could have become acquainted with it from
that source.

A fourth liturgical alteration that may be ascribed to
reaction against Christians is the omission of the Decalogue
in the synagogue service of worship. The Ten Commandments were indeed recited in the temple (Tamid 5.1), but
they were dropped in the synagogue service. According to
j. Berakhoth 1.8 this happened because of the craftiness (or,
captiousness) of the heretics (מפני טענת המינים), that is, in
order to prevent the heretics from saying that only these ten
commandments were given to Moses on Sinai. That reflects
the Christian affirmation that only the moral law had
permanent validity, while the obligation of the ceremonial

law was removed in Christ. The passage b. Berakhoth 12a,[29] admittedly somewhat unclear, suggests that in the Diaspora there were some—perhaps Jewish Christians—who wished to reintroduce the Ten Commandments.

The increasing aversion of the rabbis to the study of Greek language and literature is easily understandable in a period in which the Jews had suffered so much from the Romans and Greeks. But it is not unrelated to the debates between Jews and Christians. There is an important passage in the Mishnah which must be mentioned here. Unfortunately, it exists in two forms. The printed text of Sotah 9.14 reads:

> During the war of Titus they forbade the crowns of the brides and that a man should teach his son Greek (Danby).

But the important Cambridge manuscript has, instead of Titus, Quietus (i.e., L. Quietus, who was in Palestine *c.* 117). This reading and the date corresponding with it must be preferred. The Mishnah mentions 'the War of Vespasian', 'the War of Titus (or Quietus)', and 'The last war' (i.e. the rebellion at the time of Bar Cocheba). In this context it would be impossible to distinguish between Vespasian and Titus, and Quietus serves as a more suitable middle point than Titus. But the fact that the reference is to Quietus makes this statement all the more relevant, for between 117 and the time of the composition of the Fourth Gospel lay no great span of time. And a final step taken in the year 117 is understandable only as the culmination of ever-increasing irritation and hostility. Schlatter[30] conjectured—perhaps correctly—that the prohibition pertained only to Greek literature and rhetoric, not to the Greek language. The difference is small, for language, apart from the language of commerce, is of significance only in the realm of literature, and we may see the background of this decision in Jewish disapproval of the LXX. This disapproval is partly explained

by the exegetical debates between Jews and Christians
which are known to us from Justin's *Dialogue with Trypho*.
That the Septuagint translates עלמה as παρθένος in Isa. 7.14
is a frequently cited instance of a group of problems which
arose from the use of the Greek Old Testament. Justin
(*Trypho* 39) maintains that the Jews hate the Christians on
account of their interpretation of scripture: οὐδὲν θαυμαστὸν
εἰ καὶ ἡμᾶς μισεῖτε τοὺς ταῦτα νοοῦντας καὶ ἐλέγχοντας ὑμῶν
τὴν ἀεὶ σκληροκαρδίαν γνώμην.

We may now take a third step. We are attempting to
describe the Judaism of the Johannine period in its contacts
with Christianity. In the *Dialogue* of Justin there is much
worthwhile material of which a good deal is relevant to
our interests. I hesitate to draw upon the *Dialogue*, however,
for it is perhaps fifty years later than the gospel[31] and represents a later stage of the relationship between Jews and
Christians. A considerably earlier stage is recognizable in the
letters of Ignatius. I shall therefore begin with the doubtless
obscure but certainly important passage in *Philadelphians* 8.
(Fuller particulars may be found in the works of Lightfoot[32]
and Bauer.[33]) Ignatius puts a high premium on unity, and
one may suppose that unity was endangered in Philadelphia.
Forgiveness is offered to all penitents if they only turn to the
unity of God and to the counsel of the bishop, i.e., to the
church which assembles itself around the bishop: everything
must be done as we have learned it from Christ (κατὰ
χριστομαθίαν). In this context Ignatius mentions an event,
which had doubtless once been the source of a conflict which
he means to settle. Certain people, whom he does not more
closely describe, have made the assertion, 'If I do not find it
in the archives, I do not believe in the Gospel' (ἐὰν μὴ ἐν
τοῖς ἀρχείοις εὕρω, ἐν τῷ εὐαγγελίῳ οὐ πιστεύω). The meaning
is not clear. According to Zahn[34] 'Gospel' is in apposition to
'archives': 'If I do not find it in the archives, that is, in the
Gospel, I do not believe it.' That is, however, an improbable

rendering of the Greek. Bauer[35] translates: 'If I do not find
it in the archives, I do not believe it simply as a part of
the Gospel.' That is, what is found only in the Gospel and
not in the Old Testament is not to be believed. That, however, is somewhat too free, and πιστεύειν ἐν τῷ εὐαγγελίῳ is
not really as difficult as Bauer thinks—compare, for example,
Mark 1.15. The simplest and probably the correct translation is the one given above, which produces the sense:
'If I do not find the Gospel in the Old Testament, I do not
believe in the Gospel.'[36] That is essentially the position of
Trypho. The answer of Ignatius corresponds to it: Γέγραπται.
That is, the Christian truth as I understand it, the Gospel,
stands written in the archives, in the Old Testament. But his
opponents are not yet convinced: πρόκειται, they say—
That is just the question. At this point Ignatius breaks off the
argument, and, if we understand this section correctly, gives
up the attempt to convince his opponents, saying that Jesus
Christ, his cross, his death, his resurrection, faith in him—
these are sufficient archives for him. In other words, I seek
and value confirmation of the Gospel through the Old
Testament, but I do not need it. There is here an important
point of Christian theology, although there is some question
whether Ignatius comprehended it correctly. It is the New
Testament, with its direct witness to the cross, death, and
resurrection of Jesus, which interprets the Old Testament
and imparts meaning to it, and not the other way round.
The Old Testament does not define the meaning of the New.

That Ignatius thinks in this way is confirmed by another
passage in the same letter. In *Philadelphians* 5.2 he writes:

> And the prophets also we love (ἀγαπῶμεν), because their
> preaching also was directed towards the Gospel (εἰς τὸ εὐαγγέλ-
> ιον), and they hope in him and wait for him; they believed
> in him and were saved, being in unity with Jesus Christ.

He argues in this manner: We Christians also—like the
Jews—love and honour the prophets, but we—unlike the

Jews—hold that the prophets are incomplete in themselves; they point to Christ and find salvation only through faith in him.

9.1 is still clearer:

He is the door of the Father, through which enter Abraham and Isaac and Jacob and the prophets and the apostles and the church. All these things are joined in the unity of God.

All must enter through the same door; the heroes of the Old Testament have no private access to the Father independent of Christ.

Still other references to Jews who disturb the peace of the churches may be found in Ignatius' letters. It is impossible, however, to review all these passages.[37] We shall make an exception in one case, however, because its difficulty may be at least partly relieved by the observations just made. *Philadelphians* 6.1 begins with the warning: 'If anyone interprets ($\dot{\epsilon}\rho\mu\eta\nu\epsilon\dot{\upsilon}\eta$) Judaism to you, do not listen to him!' $\dot{\epsilon}\rho\mu\eta\nu\epsilon\dot{\upsilon}\epsilon\iota\nu$ is probably to be understood in the light of what has been said earlier about the prophets: 'Listen to no one who interprets the prophets in purely Jewish fashion and not in relation to their fulfilment in Christ.' Ignatius continues: 'For it is better to listen to Christianity from a circumcised man than to Judaism from an uncircumcised man.' The first part of the sentence is clear: a Jew can be converted to Christianity and then preach Christianity. Is there reflected also in Ignatius a tendency to disparage such a man? That is possible, but not important; the circumcised Christian thinks and acts in an essentially orthodox way. But what uncircumcised person preaches or can preach Judaism? The matter is important, because it allows us to think that there existed a syncretistic Judaism, about which we shall have more to say later.[38] If the words of Ignatius are not merely a rhetorical, parallelizing form, they could indicate an unusual form of Judaism, a Judaism in the process of transformation into a new religion which would no longer require the maintenance of such material conditions of Judaism as circumcision. The same idea is suggested in another rather unclear statement (*Magnesians* 10.3):

> It is out of the question to talk of Jesus Christ and to practise Judaism (ἰουδαΐζειν). For Christianity did not believe in Judaism, but Judaism in Christianity.

A syncretistic Judaism is resisted in this passage also.

There are also several places, in which Ignatius attacks a Gnosis which expressed docetic views of the person of Jesus and similar views of the Lord's Supper. *Ephesians* 17 is significant although here the docetic question is not addressed directly:

> Be not anointed with the evil odour of the doctrine of the Prince of this age (τοῦ ἄρχοντος τοῦ αἰῶνος τούτου) . . . Why are we not all prudent (φρόνιμοι) seeing that we have received knowledge of God (θεοῦ γνῶσιν), that is, Jesus Christ?

The description of this false teaching recalls a sort of Gnosis over against which Ignatius[39] maintains that each Christian has received knowledge of God in Christ, and is, or should be, wise.

Most scholars are agreed[40] that Ignatius speaks of only one group of opponents rather than two. This opinion must, however, be qualified in so far as we have to bear in mind that the opposition he encountered may have differed from place to place. Some important passages combine the respective accusations and groups so closely that it is very difficult to distinguish them. For example, in *Magnesians* 8 Ignatius warns his readers not to be led astray by heresies and fables (μυθεύματα). That sounds like Gnosis, but he continues:

> For if we are living until now according to Judaism, we confess that we have not received grace.

He adds that one calls in vain on the prophets to support the false teaching: For the divine prophets lived according to Jesus Christ. Probably the Gnostic opponents had appealed to the prophets.

Smyrnaeans 5 also has in view docetists, who probably are Jews, since they are accused of not paying attention to the prophets and the law, that is, they understand the prophets and the law otherwise than does Ignatius. Also *Smyrnaeans* 7 (Lightfoot, 6) makes a similar connection: There are some who refrain from the Eucharist; for they do not recognize it as the flesh of our Lord Jesus Christ, which flesh has suffered on account of our sins and been raised by the Father. Such people, Ignatius advises, we should avoid, and rather attend to the prophets—naturally, as Ignatius interprets them, on the basis of his understanding of the Gospel.

We may therefore maintain that Ignatius encountered persons, probably in his native Antioch and in the Asian churches, who, although probably not identical in every locality, could be described as having both Jewish and Gnostic tendencies. That does not mean that they were Jewish Gnostics in the sense of Jews who had accepted a Gnostic interpretation of Judaism, for some of them were not circumcised. Probably they had attained their faith through Christianity. It may be supposed that in Asia Christianity, Judaism, and Gnosis existed alongside one another and that they became intermingled with one another. This conclusion, to which the Ignatian letters lead, is important, especially since it is supported by allusions to Judaism in the seven letters of the Apocalypse of John. The author of the Apocalypse knows that there are in Smyrna people who claim to be Jews, but in fact are a synagogue of Satan (2.9). He knows that in Thyatira there is a woman who claims to be a prophetess, although she seduces the church members into lewdness and the eating of forbidden foods (2.20), a woman whose activity is related to the 'deep things' of Satan (2.24). Philadelphia also has its fraudulent Jews (3.9). In this category should perhaps be placed the followers of Balaam (2.14) and the Nicolaitans (2.6,15).

We have now indicated some important features in the picture of the Judaism of the Johannine period. It is true that up to this point I have said nothing about the Qumran scrolls. There is a reason for this omission. In the first place, it seems to me that the similarities between the Fourth Gospel and the Qumran literature have been overstated at the expense of their differences, which are almost or quite as important. In the second place, we must take into consideration the question of the date of composition. Not only were all the Qumran scrolls written before 70, but the community of Qumran ceased to exist at this time;[41] thus at the time when the gospel was composed the community no longer existed. In spite of this, however, it is entirely possible that some of the concepts which we find in the literature lived on thereafter.[42]

I should not wish, on the basis of these propositions, to draw the conclusion that the Qumran literature is of no relevance to the Fourth Gospel. The parallels collected by K. G. Kuhn,[43] H. Braun,[44] and R. E. Brown[45] could in individual cases be called into question, but it is scarcely possible to discount them all.[46] Thus, it is not to be denied that the scrolls show a decided interest in 'knowledge' and in apparently dualistic pairs such as light and darkness. This interest confirms the conjecture already made, i.e. that Hellenistic and Gnostic ways of thinking had already penetrated Palestine. In these complexes there is certainly a parallel to the Fourth Gospel, which also shows an interest in knowledge and in dualistically related pairs. But in the scrolls there is not only this Gnosticism—or Gnosis, or pseudo-Gnosticism, or proto-Gnosticism. There is also much besides. Thus one recalls, for example, the detailed and strict rules for the life of a community which deemed itself obliged to shut itself off from the world and to follow a fixed liturgical and disciplinary order. Of all this the Fourth Gospel shows no trace. In that gospel there is, in fact, a group of friends or brothers; but they live within the world and not outside it (17.15). Moreover, they receive only one commandment, that they love one another (15.12). They submit to no liturgical obligations. Their interrelations are regulated by no law and sanctioned by no punishment. Their single bond of unity is Jesus himself. They live in separation from the world only in the sense that they are Jesus' disciples. The particular Qumran regulations express in a distinctive way the essentially legal foundation of Judaism. On the other hand, John, although he did not hold the law of Moses in contempt, regarded it as of secondary importance in comparison with grace and truth, which have come through Christ (1.17).

Among the Qumran documents, the commentaries, which follow the pesher method, are extremely important. John also reveres and uses the Old Testament, even though it could not be expected that he should include a commentary in his gospel. Yet his treatment of the Old Testament is both formally and thematically different from that of the scrolls.[47] Finally, one observes that in the scrolls the dualistic metaphors are employed not only for religious but also for political and military purposes. On the one hand, the War Scroll is an apocalyptic drama which deals with a fantasy-war. On the other, it is also based upon the observation of actual military practice[48] and looks forward to a real, if also partially supernatural, victory of the Sons of Light over the Sons of Darkness. It scarcely need be added that 'light' and 'darkness' are used differently in the Fourth Gospel.

In the very nature of the case, the Qumran community and its literature and theology came to an end in the year 70. For our purposes they are, nevertheless, very important. They show that a non-Jewish world of thought could influence even zealous nationalistic Jewish groups. Further-more, they show that non-Jewish ideas could in such groups be given new life in a manner in accord with the Old Testament model, so that 'dualism' becomes 'qualified dualism', and 'light' and 'darkness' are no longer absolute and eternally opposed antitheses, but creations of the one God who remains ever the Lord.

Because of considerations of time, we must limit ourselves to a very brief summary, in order to be able to set out from it at the beginning of the next lecture. It does not suffice to say that the Fourth Gospel is either Jewish or Hellenistic. It is both. In so far as it is Jewish, we must go on to ask: To what form of Judaism is it related? and then, What is that relationship? We have now very briefly looked into the first question; the second remains before us. Of the Judaism of the last decade of the first century we may only say: (*a*) that this period—with few exceptions—saw the end of Jewish apocalyptic, for this expression of Jewish faith had fulfilled its purpose; (*b*) that Gnostic concepts had already before 70 penetrated Judaism, as Qumran shows, but the gnosticizing of Judaism continued, and, indeed, in those circles in which Judaism came into contact with Christianity (Ignatius); (*c*) that at the same time a new institutional development began, for after the fall of the temple increased emphasis was laid upon those ordinances whose execution was not bound to the temple, and it was these which furthered the cohesiveness of the nation and strengthened it against the threat of heresy and disintegration.

All of this is important for the investigation of the Fourth Gospel, as we shall now further attempt to show.

4

The Fourth Gospel and
Judaism

In the first three lectures we could only sketch three broad problem areas. Each might have been dealt with in much greater detail. It was possible only to call attention to several of the questions which are raised by our main theme, as well as to indicate some of the lines which more detailed subsequent investigations must follow. I hope, nevertheless, at least to have made clear that some previous attempts to relate the gospel to Judaism have been unsuccessful because matters have been too simply put.

From the standpoint we have reached it is both easy and correct to say that Torrey,[1] Burney,[2] and others came much too quickly to their position that the Fourth Gospel is a translation from Aramaic into Greek. Today we may say with certainty that this is not so; the Fourth Gospel is a Greek book.

On the other hand, it is also important not to overlook the Semitic ring of the language of the gospel, and its importance should not be underestimated. How has this Semitic ring come into the Johannine Greek? It does not suffice to say that it is strongest in sayings ascribed to Jesus and John the Baptist. That would indeed be a convenient explanation, but the Semitic colouring is a trait of the uniform style of the entire gospel. Thus, it appears in the Prologue. Even if there may also have been a special source containing words of

Jesus and the Baptist, we must see in the Semitisms an essential hallmark of the evangelist himself. Jewish language is in some measure a characteristic of the gospel and is to be explained in connection with its environment and purpose.[3]

In a similar way, it is both easy and correct to say that Albright[4] and others have built too much on somewhat ambiguous topographical and archaeological data. Here and there the Johannine data seem to agree with other evidence concerning Palestinian localities, especially as regards Jerusalem. But one may not draw the conclusion that John writes in order to transmit such information. He should certainly not be read as an ancient Baedeker. On the other hand, he has no occasion to omit or deny the traditional connection of certain events with Cana, Capernaum, Sychar, or Gabbatha. Such place names, which as a rule have no theological significance, are doubtless taken from old tradition. Whether they are historically correct or not depends on how one evaluates that tradition and cannot be discussed here. What is impossible to maintain is that this material has a positive purpose. Rather, it appears in the gospel more or less by chance. It should be recalled, moreover, that in many respects John contradicts the Synoptic Gospels, so that both cannot be right. One may say only that the evangelist no more intends to emphasize the historical elements tying his narrative to the Palestine in which Jesus lived than he intends to set them aside.

If one turns to the material content of the gospel, similar observations may be made. William Temple, admittedly not a New Testament scholar, before the discovery of the Qumran documents expressed himself quite boldly: 'The Gospel is through and through Palestinian. The notion that it is in any sense Hellenistic is contrary to its whole tenour.'[5] It should not be overlooked, however, that on the next page Temple nearly contradicts himself. He writes that in the prologue 'the term "Logos" is used in its Hellenistic as well as its Jewish sense, as a medium of interpretation to the Greek-speaking people of Ephesus'.[6] But even this is an entirely unsatisfactory qualification, for the adjective 'Palestinian' does not itself mean 'non-Hellenistic', since Palestine was a part of the Roman Empire and thus of the Hellenistic world. In any case one may ask: How could a book written in Greek be in no sense Hellenistic (or Hellenic)? The Jewish literature which we have in Greek dress is the product of Hellenistic Judaism. Even if the Fourth Gospel were exclusively Jewish, one would have to consider it Hellenistic–Jewish.

Logos, however, is by no means the only word in the Fourth Gospel which has not only a Jewish, but also a Hellenistic ring. A comparison between the Johannine vocabulary and that of the Gospel of Truth[7] has shown that John was acquainted with the questions raised by Gnosticism. Yet despite such interconnections with Gnosticism and other forms of Hellenism, the Palestinian or—better—the essentially Jewish elements in the distinctive character of the Fourth Gospel must be recognized. In my opinion we must take seriously John's real interest in the events which took place in Palestine.[8] Moreover, we grant that he regarded these events not as distant occurrences, but as events which still at the end of the century determined the existence of mankind.[9] Therefore, they were, or should be, intelligible to later generations. In order that they might retain their intelligibility, they required reinterpretation, but not complete transformation. It is clear enough that the background and environment of the Fourth Gospel were in a certain sense Jewish, but that they were Jewish only in part. Equally important is the fact that those originally Jewish elements (that is, those events which took place in Palestine among men who thought, spoke, and acted as Jews) have received a later, non-Jewish form through reinterpretation.

On similar grounds one cannot be satisfied with the

seemingly opposite opinion that the gospel was basically a
Gnostic work and has been somewhat Christianized. This
position can be presented in a very convincing way but it is
only partially, and not exclusively, correct. If, for example,
the Johannine concept of knowledge is investigated thoroughly, one can scarcely avoid the conclusion that Bultmann
has failed to find the correct explanation of a state of affairs
which he has described better than any other commentator.[10]
There is a difference between the Gnostic and Old Testament theories· of knowledge. It is, however, preferable to
think that John drew upon both rather than that he inde-
pendently transformed the Gnostic theory into something
very similar to the Old Testament.[11] Here, as well as in other
areas which I have mentioned,[12] it seems to me that one
commentator after another has described some features of
the gospel with a clarity and forcefulness which he was able
to acquire only by closing his eyes to others.

The same observation could be made about many other
attempts to define the purpose of the evangelist. Because
Dodd[13] directs his attention to the Greek elements in the
gospel, he can maintain that it was written to win converts
from among the adherents of the higher pagan religions.
Van Unnik[14] focuses upon Jewish messianism and can thus
maintain that the purpose of the author was to win over the
synagogues of the Diaspora. Lightfoot[15] notes that the gospel
is dependent upon earlier Christian tradition and reinter-
prets it; therefore, he describes the gospel as 'the verdict of
history, or perhaps we should rather say the verdict of the
Church, on the Lord's Person and work'. Therefore, it is
a book written mainly for Christians in order to show them
the full significance of their faith. I believe that the impartial
reader will conclude that here, as so often, enthusiastic
scholars appear not so much blind in the face of inconvenient
facts as sensitive to those facts which are favourable to their
particular goals. The result is that one finds more truth in

what they affirm than in what they deny. But that leads to a very general conclusion, which could apply to any sphere of historical research. To speak more precisely, therefore, the students of this gospel have too often seen a part or some parts of the whole, but not all the parts, above all, not all the parts in their proper relation to one another.

Precisely at this point our consideration of Judaism, limited as it may be, gains its urgency and relevance. The reader who opens C. H. Dodd's *Interpretation of the Fourth Gospel*[16] finds in the first part of the book an outstanding account of various aspects of the ancient world. No one could hold that account and its author in greater respect than I do. But let us look more closely at the two chapters which deal with Judaism. The first bears the title 'Hellenistic Judaism: Philo of Alexandria'. Actually, the chapter is devoted to Philo, and Dodd comes to what is doubtless the correct conclusion when he writes: 'It seems clear, therefore, that . . . the Fourth Gospel . . . certainly presupposes a range of ideas having a remarkable resemblance to those of Hellenistic Judaism as represented by Philo.'[17] The difficulty consists in the fact that Philo died about a half-century before the composition of the gospel. It would be foolish to maintain that Philo had no successors or that his world of thought died with him. The transmission of his writings proves that they were admired and read. But times change, things pass off the scene, and the needs and interests of people change. The time between 1917 and 1967 also comprehends a half-century! Before this comparison is rejected as irrelevant, one should remember that the half-century between the death of Philo and John saw a revolution and one of the bloodiest of wars, namely, the supersession of the Julio-Claudian Emperors by the Flavians and the four-year war of 66–70 which resulted in the downfall of an ancient state.

The second chapter, which deals with the Jewish background of the gospel, is entitled 'Rabbinic Judaism'. Any discussion of this subject encounters the difficulty that the material originated over a very long period of time. Now Dodd is in fact considerably more careful than many others; so far as possible, he dates the rabbinic passages which he cites. For example, he concludes the section on 'The Name of God' with this comment:

> Much of this will seem somewhat speculative, and the links in the chain of evidence are not all complete, but it is at least possible that one of the most distinctive ideas of the Fourth Gospel, and one which has been thought most remote from the Judaism within which Christianity arose, has its roots in reflections of Jewish Rabbis upon prophetic teaching about the relation between God and His people, in the light of the disasters which fell upon Israel during the period A.D. 70–135.[18]

This is a very perceptive remark, one which points out the path I should hope to follow. One must concede, however, that this method is not carried through consistently by Dodd himself, for he frequently uses material from a later period and in general appears to be satisfied to consider the Judaism of the first century as a whole, as though what applied to the time of Jesus applied equally to the time of John, although the one lies more than a generation before A.D. 70 and the other almost a generation after.

Naturally, I have no intention of depreciating the excellence and significance of Dodd's work; but I do believe that the time has come to take a step further. The scope of these four lectures, in which I attempt to survey the general area, does not permit us to take this step. It may, however, be useful at least to indicate the main lines of any further advance.

In the Fourth Gospel the perplexing series of relations to various major religious streams and tendencies of antiquity is noteworthy. The gospel stands in relation to Greek thought, admittedly not to the classical philosophical systems, but to the eclectic religious philosophy which was practised in the first century by the pious—too religious to be rationalist, and too rationalist to be religious in the popular sense. From here it is a matter of only a single, but necessary, step to the conclusion that the gospel is also related to Gnosticism.[19] I believe that both views are right; the gospel is related both to eclectic philosophy and to Gnosticism. But both positions must, as I have already indicated,[20] grapple with difficulties: contemporary sources for such philosophy and for Gnosticism are not easy to find. This objection has been raised in particular against Bultmann's theory of a Gnostic base for the gospel. Even where the presence of a sort of proto-Gnosis in New Testament times is conceded, it is pointed out that there is no pre-Christian text which contains the myth of the descending and ascending revealer and redeemer.[21] Even the Hermetic writings, upon which Dodd relies so heavily, are later than the New Testament. Dodd dates them as early as possible, but there nevertheless remains an interval to be reckoned with.

Now the investigator reckons with such time gaps in ancient history and attempts to fill them in. It becomes, however, even more important to make full use of our knowledge of Judaism. But we are also unable to write a complete history of the Judaism of this epoch. Not many Jewish books were composed between 70 and 100, and although Josephus may be added to the few surviving apocalypses, his history breaks off exactly at the point at which we need it most. We have, however, attempted to indicate some characteristics of the period, and these earlier observations must now be reiterated.

At the end of the third lecture I enumerated the identifying marks of Judaism in the Johannine period.[22] These were: (*a*) the disappearance of apocalyptic; (*b*) the advent of Gnosis; (*c*) the advance of institutionalism. In part these developments took place in opposition to Christianity, but parallel developments within Christianity may also be noted.

This observation is of extraordinary importance. Relations between Judaism and Christianity are in general marked by this opposition and parallelism, so that this twofold, paradoxical relation between the two religions becomes decisive for their historical and theological relationship. In the Fourth Gospel it plays a special role, and therefore it must be analysed further.

In Christianity as well as in Judaism apocalyptic had suffered staggering reversals. The original apocalyptic hopes had twice been disappointed: at the crucifixion of Jesus God had not intervened;[23] moreover, the hope which developed later, that the parousia of the Son of man would take place before the end of the first Christian generation, was similarly disappointed. The Fathers had fallen asleep, and the promise of his coming was delayed (2 Pet. 3.4). No longer could apocalyptic serve as a suitable medium for Christian faith, as it once did. Admittedly, this led to the disappearance of apocalyptic only within a narrow circle. The composition of the Apocalypse of John shows that the hope for an early return of the Lord lived on.[24] In Judaism the motivation was admittedly different. Only with difficulty could one separate apocalyptic from the nationalism which had been grievously shaken in the year 70 and had received its death blow in 135. As in Christianity there was also in Judaism, along with the preservation of a generalized future expectation, a sporadic outbreak of apocalyptic fervour and elsewhere a dying out of this interest.

To the decline of apocalyptic Judaism and Christianity reacted in a twofold way. There was both a crystallization of institutions and of legal demands and also at the same time a willingness to accept Gnostic ways of thinking. Both traits may be traced in Christianity[25] as well as in Judaism[26] before 70, but in both religions they developed further in the following decades. By the passing of time Christians were forced to recognize that the end of the ages had not come and that their faith had to wait for an indefinite future. Therefore they endeavoured to create a defence, so far as institutions and rules could accomplish it: a formally instituted ministry developed; the concept of orthodoxy began to harden; the danger of an understanding of the Gospel as another law lay ever near.[27] In Judaism the new situation which we have already discussed was brought about by the war of 66–70. Even if the temple area was not allowed to stand wholly unused,[28] Judaism had now as never before (except in isolated pietistic groups) to rely upon the synagogue and upon that form of legalism presented in finished form in the Mishnah.

It would be superficial to maintain that institutionalism and Gnosis were alternative ways of overcoming the demise of apocalyptic, as if belief in the nearness of the coming age or the end of history could either harden into the form of an institution dispensing salvation or dissolve into the spiritual enthusiasm of a private Gnostic religion. One may see an either–or of this sort in the Christianity of the second century; the Catholic church ranged itself against all Gnostic tendencies. But in the Johannine period it was different. Even Ignatius, that earnest defender of the threefold ministry of the church, represents a theology of a decidedly Gnostic type,[29] while at the same time opposing the erroneous teaching of Jewish docetism. The anti-Gnostic author of the Pastoral Letters can cite a hymn about the Redeemer who descends in order to manifest himself in the flesh and ascends in order to be glorified in heaven (1 Tim. 3.16). If one may define early Catholicism as 'the defensive movement of the church against threatening Gnosticism',[30] one must also recognize[31] that the earliest early Catholicism was in a certain sense influenced by Gnosticism. On the other hand, in Judaism the rabbinic development of a religion of law was accompanied by a strand of rabbinic mysticism.[32]

Our thesis is therefore confirmed: between the development of Judaism and of Christianity at the end of the first century a certain parallelism can be established. There was a mutual assimilation; there were even men for whom there were not two religions, Judaism and Christianity, but only one, Jewish Christianity. These men were not all Jews; we have already learned from Ignatius that it was possible to hear Judaism from an uncircumcised man. The material which we can glean from the letters of Ignatius is sufficient to enable us to draw a picture of such Jewish Christians. Since we have already given such a sketch, we do not need to repeat it.[33] There is also additional material, although it is not easy to utilize, quite apart from the fact that its history can be reconstructed only hypothetically. To what extent, for example, may the Clementine literature be used to describe a movement older than that literature itself? Here, without discussing the problem in detail, I may simply express the opinion that there are sufficient grounds to postulate the presence of a movement of Christian, Jewish, Gnostic, and strongly anti-Pauline character. An earlier form of this movement is opposed in the Pastoral Letters. We may here recall that O. Cullmann has attempted to prove that after the defeat of 70 the remnants of the Qumran community went over to Christianity.[34] Cullmann writes somewhat boldly:[35] 'In matters of detail we can only advance hypotheses. On the other hand, the position that after the year 70 remnants of the Qumran sect passed over into Jewish Christianity is more than an hypothesis.' Even if greater caution is desirable in the matter, there is still no reason why this hypothesis must necessarily be false. In Justin's time the Jewish Christians had already lost the battle. It is possible, however, to trace in Justin's position an earlier situation in which Jewish Christians had attempted to impose their Jewish customs upon Gentile Christians.[36]

In the last decades of the first century and the first decades of the second Judaism had to fight for its life. The military operations of 115–16 and 135 show that this was so. More

was at stake than military success and political independence. The latter was actually lost, but Judaism lived on.
The real danger lay in the loss of religious independence, the
possibility that Judaism would simply assimilate itself to
other religions; in this regard Christianity posed the gravest
threat. At least two reactions to this danger may be observed.
The one consisted in complete rejection and separation.
The *Birkath ha-minim*[37] excluded Jewish Christians from the
liturgy and therefore from the life of the synagogue and the
Jewish community. The name of Jesus was forbidden as a
means of healing;[38] sayings of Jesus might not be quoted,
much less approved.[39] The second reaction consisted simply
in the incorporation of Christianity into Judaism; this
reaction produced the Judaism which we have already
briefly described.[40]

The fact is that there was a continuing relation between
Christianity and Judaism which involved both attraction and
repulsion. During the subsequent centuries this relationship
has frequently been misunderstood—too often with tragic
consequences. The time which I have called the Johannine
period saw the first effects of this relation. Paul[41] indeed
understood the relation very well; but it was only after 70
that it had to find practical expression. By then the similarities and dissimilarities of the two religions could be
seen with full clarity. Previously they had been concealed
by the fact that one of them was not only a religion, but
also a state, while the other was not yet completely
separate from it. The Jews hoped to keep the Christians
within the state; the Christians hoped for the conversion of
all Jews.

We are now perhaps in a position to understand somewhat
better the subject 'The Gospel of John and Judaism'.

The Jewish traits of the Gospel of John are well known;
every textbook contains a list of them.[42] There are the use
of the Old Testament, Jewish terminology, Semitic terms,

rabbinic exegesis, place names, and now the parallels with the Qumran writings. All of this is important.

Also important, and not unrecognized, are the anti-Jewish traits. These are clearly seen in the often pejorative references to the Jews:

> 5.16 Therefore the Jews persecuted Jesus.
> 10.31 The Jews took up stones again to stone him.
> 18.36 If my kingship were of this world, my servants would fight, that I might not be handed over to the Jews.

Clearly 'the Jews' form a group antagonistic to Jesus. The same impression is conveyed by references to the law as something from which both Jesus and the evangelist dissociate themselves:

> 10.34 Is it not written in your law . . .?
> 15.25 It is to fulfil the word that is written in their law, 'They hated me without a cause.'
> 19.7 The Jews answered him. 'We have a law, and by that law he ought to die, because he made himself the Son of God.'

Such passages could have been written only by someone who was consciously standing outside Judaism. Of course, he may once have been a Jew. In the Fourth Gospel there is nothing stronger than the sayings of the Jew Paul: To the Jews I became as a Jew (1 Cor. 9.20); and: Christ is the end of the Law (Rom. 10.4). But the evangelist may also have ceased to be a Jew in that he became ἀποσυνάγωγος (9.22; 16.2)—not by his own desire, but by command of the synagogue. According to John the Jewish opposition to Christianity had reached such a that pitch capital punishment was administered in the name of God (16.2). John could not pay back in the same coin, but he could maintain that his Jewish opponents were descended not from Abraham but from the devil, and that in their opposition they performed the works of the devil (8.44). Opposition against Christians was the result of an earlier decision against Jesus, who was deemed to have been born out of wedlock (8.41) and possessed of a demon (8.48). He was no real Jew (8.48) and he had made for himself false and blasphemous claims (5.18; 19.7). With respect to Jesus, Jews and Christians could only contradict one another.

John's anti-Jewish attitude becomes particularly clear in the Passion Narrative. In the trial of Jesus the Jews seize the initiative. It is astonishing, therefore, that the Romans rather than the Jews arrest Jesus; but Jesus is not first brought to the governor but to Annas and Caiaphas. In the Jewish court the procedure must be illegal (18.19–23). Pilate attempts to free Jesus and declares that the captive is guiltless. When, however, the Jews threaten him with an accusation which he could scarcely answer, he agrees to the Jewish demand for execution, and does so in such a way that the Jews themselves are driven to blasphemy: οὐκ ἔχομεν βασιλέα εἰ μὴ Καίσαρα (19.15). It is not necessary to accept all the conclusions of P. Winter[43]—although many may be correct—to perceive here a distortion of history, and it is perhaps not so important to decide whether the distortion was conscious or developed unconsciously with the increasing enmity between Christians and Jews during that period.

The fact is that this gospel contains Judaism, non-Judaism, and anti-Judaism. It remains to be asked how this mixture of motivations and prejudices is to be understood in relation to the environment of the work. It has been conjectured that the gospel reflects debates in the synagogue of the Diaspora. It is certain that such debates took place, and it is not improbable that the evangelist participated in them. But this hypothesis does not suffice unless we suppose that John himself played the roles of Christian, of Jew, and of Greek listener.

John is both Jewish and anti-Jewish. That means not only that he possessed the human virtue of being able to see the good in all men, even Jews, or that he had the intellectual virtue of being able to comprehend both sides of a theological argument. He could at the same time write: 'Salvation is of the Jews' (4.22), and: 'You are from your father, the devil, and you will to do according to his desires' (8.44). These are not the contradictory assertions of two parties in a debate. Jesus himself says both things. The evangelist says both. Both are true. These Johannine tendencies, the Jewish and the anti-Jewish, are not to be adjudged unharmonized tendencies of different sources, nor are they to be explained as the product of fortuitous historical circumstances. They arise out of the Johannine understanding of the dialectic of Christian truth. That this is the case derives from the fact that such antitheses are especially characteristic of John. That the antitheses are deliberate and not the chance product of literary endeavour is shown in this fundamental case. I cannot at this point undertake an exposition of the whole Gospel, but without forgetting the special theme of John and Judaism, I must briefly go into the most important Johannine antitheses in order to provide a framework within which that theme may be understood.

John combines Gnosis and anti-Gnosticism. This fact has been frequently noticed. The noun γνῶσις does not appear in the gospel, but the verbs γινώσκειν and εἰδέναι are extraordinarily frequent and are used by John to express his main theme. In this connection one notices especially 17.3: 'This is eternal life, that they should know thee, the only true God, and Jesus Christ whom thou didst send.' Many other passages could be cited. Salvation comes through knowing, yet salvation consists not of knowledge but of love.

The conclusion of the seventeenth chapter summarizes the theme:

> Righteous Father, the world did not know thee, but I knew thee; and these men have come to know that thou didst send me.

(In this verse [17.25] the most significant Gnostic themes
appear: knowledge and the sending of the heavenly emissary.
John continues:)

> I have made known to them thy name, and I will make it
> known, that the love with which thou hast loved me may be in
> them, and I in them.

The final goal is not, therefore, Gnosis or wisdom, but
love. Love is the hallmark of the disciples of Jesus (13.35), as
it is also the divine motivation for the mission of the Son
(3.16). This is a most important observation. It is also to be
noticed, however, that John uses Gnostic language in a non-
Gnostic sense. The dualistic pairs such as light and darkness
are not actually dualistic, that is, they do not signify absolute,
eternal antitheses, but are a linguistic means of expressing deliverance, judgement, and decision. We cannot here go
into the question whether John used a Gnostic source and
Christianized it. That is certainly possible; yet it is equally
possible that John himself reinterpreted and reformulated
the Christian tradition in Gnostic terminology. It is more
important, however, that in this gospel Gnosis is not simply
rejected, but modified and counterbalanced by non-Gnostic
material. This does not mean that John could not decide
for one thing or the other; the dialectic of love and Gnosis is
precisely what he wished to express.

John combines apocalyptic with non-apocalyptic material.
In this regard the gospel is very often oversimplified. John
gave up the expectation of an imminent parousia of the Son
of man, but that does not mean that he no longer looked in
hope to the future. For him eschatology is realized in the
present, but not so completely that the future is no longer of
any significance. For John there is no historical moment
which is self-explanatory—not the present moment of mysti-
cal or churchly experience, not even the historical moment
of the activity of Jesus. There remains a last day[44] (John

6.39,40,44,54). Even if the Christian eats the flesh of the Son of man, drinks his blood, and thereby has life in himself, he does not have it in such a way that he is from now on an independent source of life. It is still necessary that Jesus should raise him from the dead at the last day. John may have recognized that apocalyptic language[45] was unavoidable; to give it up would be to falsify the Christian faith. He retains it and reworks it, as he retains and reworks Gnostic language. The emphasis lies more upon a modified present eschatology than upon the future, but the latter—yet not in the sense of imminent expectation—is present in the gospel, and precisely the coexistence of both is important for Johannine theology. To set out to dissolve this coexistence through source or redaction hypotheses is methodologically false.[46]

John combines a deep interest in the apostolic foundation of the church with an indifference toward it as an institution dispensing salvation. Whether this combination should be described 'Early Catholicism' I do not know. Certainly it would be a very rare form of Catholicism. John does not concern himself with the form of the church. Yet he is concerned that the church should be apostolic in the sense that it should remain faithful to the teaching of the apostles. The identifying marks of the apostolic community are the word of Jesus (8.31) and love (13.35). Blessed are those who have not seen, but believe (20.29); they can, however, be blessed because others have seen and believed (20.8). This also becomes especially clear in chapter 6, in the Johannine allusions to the Lord's Supper:

> He who eats my flesh and drinks my blood has eternal life . . . For my flesh is food indeed, and my blood is drink indeed. He who eats my flesh and drinks my blood abides in me, and I in him (6.54ff).

But in 6.63 he can write:

> It is the spirit that gives life, the flesh is of no avail; the words that I have spoken to you are spirit and life.

I cannot believe that these apparently contradictory statements were left to stand side by side in the gospel because John was too careless, or too stupid, to notice an actual incompatibility. He knew very well what he was doing. Eating and drinking, important as they were, were not to be identified with a cultic rite, although it is possible that (a) they were so identified in a source which John used and (b) that John used the language of a well-known rite. Thus, as Hoskyns[47] rightly observed, John intended to bind the church to the apostolic witness; but in other respects he meant to leave it free.[48]

Such combinations and antitheses are characteristic of the Gospel of John but not of it alone; parallels are to be found in the Old Testament and in Judaism.[49] Actually, however, the paradoxical Johannine position with respect to Judaism, which John necessarily developed out of his historic circumstances, created the framework in which other combinations could exist. The historical situation in which Christianity entered into such relations with Gnosis, institutionalism, and Judaism, was certainly confusing enough. But in a similar way Judaism had to come to terms with Christianity, Gnosis, and institutionalism. Some quite amazing combinations developed before the two religions attained fixed forms, which were not the forms of earlier periods.[50] The theological situation with which John saw himself confronted, consisting as it did of the similarity and dissimilarity which existed between Christianity and Judaism, provided a model for his treatment of the problems of the closing years of the century.

It follows from these considerations that an hypothesis which, for example, understands the Fourth Gospel simply as a missionary tract for the Jews and expounds it as such, cannot be satisfactory. It can describe a part of the historical situation, but for the theological situation it is wholly insufficient. In the final reckoning, this gospel is to be explained not historically, but theologically. The merit of John does not consist in his having satisfied a passing, practical need by means of a fly-sheet,[51] but in his having known abiding elements of theological truth. These evolved out of the tension between Judaism and Christianity, but they led out beyond this original frame of reference. Thus John, with the wealth of language at his disposal, bore his witness to Jesus.

Notes

CHAPTER 1

1   B. F. Westcott, *The Gospel according to St John* (London 1881, 1903);
    also the uncompleted posthumous work with the same title (London
    1908).

2   *The Gospel according to St John* (1903), p. xviii.

3   J. Drummond, *An Inquiry into the Character and Authorship of the
    Fourth Gospel* (London 1903).

4   W. Sanday, *The Criticism of the Fourth Gospel* (Oxford 1905).

5   J. Moffatt, *An Introduction to the Literature of the New Testament* (1911;
    3e., Edinburgh 1927), p. 522.

6   Ibid., p. 570.

7   A. Schweitzer, *The Mysticism of Paul the Apostle*, tr. W. Montgomery
    (London 1931).

8   Ibid., p. 349.

9   Ibid., p. 351.

10 C. H. Dodd, *The Interpretation of the Fourth Gospel* (Cambridge 1953).

11 Ibid., p. 97.

12 Ibid., p. 114.

13 Ibid., p. 92.

14 Ibid., p. 73.

15 Ibid., p. 53.

16 Ibid., p. 9.

17 E. C. Hoskyns, *The Fourth Gospel* (London 1940), ed. F. N. Davey.

18 R. H. Lightfoot, *St John's Gospel, a Commentary* (Oxford 1956), ed.
    C. F. Evans.

19 Hoskyns, op. cit., p. xxii (in later editions, p. 108).

20 Ibid., p. xxiii (in later editions, p. 108).

21 Ibid., p. 130 (in later editions, p. 137).

22 Cf. R. H. Fuller, *The New Testament in Current Study* (New York and London 1962), p. 104, who cites E. Käsemann, but without indicating the reference.

23 *Der Römerbrief* (München 1929), p. xi (ET by E. C. Hoskyns, *The Epistle to the Romans* (London 1933), p. 7).

24 Op. cit. (München 1933), p. xx (ET, p. 16).

25 *Das Evangelium des Johannes* (Göttingen 1950; ET, Oxford 1971).

26 R. Bultmann, *Theology of the New Testament*, tr. K. Grobel, ıı (New York and London 1955), p. 13.

27 Ibid., p. 13.

28 R. McL. Wilson, *Gnosis and the New Testament* (Oxford 1968), proposes that 'Gnosticism' should be used for the Christian heresy and 'Gnosis' for the broader phenomenon. But can this distinction now be carried into effect?

29 R. Bultmann, *Primitive Christianity in its Contemporary Setting*, tr. R. H. Fuller (London and New York 1956), p. 162.

30 Too often, particularly in England, this rhetorical question is taken to be a complete answer to Bultmann; but it is certainly not.

31 *Einleitung in das Neue Testament* (Bern 1961), p. 123.

32 'The Purpose of St John's Gospel' in *Studia Evangelica* ı (Texte und Untersuchungen 73) (Berlin 1959), pp. 382–411.

33 Ibid., p. 395.

34 Justin, *Apology* ı, 31.6.

35 Van Unnik cites *Trypho* 46.1; 47.1; 39.7 (ἤδη οὖν τὸν λόγον ἀπόδος ἡμῖν, ὅτι οὗτος . . . ἐστὶν ὁ χριστὸς τοῦ θεοῦ).

36 *Studia Evangelica* ı, p. 402.

37 Ibid., p. 406.

38 Ibid., p. 410.

39 'The Destination and Purpose of St John's Gospel' in *New Testament Studies* 6 (1960), pp. 117–31.

40 Ibid., p. 130.

41 Ibid., pp. 130f.

42 'The Significance of the Qumran Texts for Research into the Beginnings of Christianity' in *Journal of Biblical Literature* 74 (1955), pp. 213–26 (reprinted in *The Scrolls and the New Testament*, ed. K. Stendahl (London 1958), pp. 18–32). Cf. 'L'Opposition contre le temple de Jérusalem, motif commun de la théologie johannique et du monde ambiant' in *New Testament Studies* 5 (1959), pp. 157–73.

43 Cullmann mentions, for example, the Johannine and Qumran rejection of the temple. But John and the Qumran community rejected the temple for different reasons: John because the true worshipper must worship in spirit and in truth (John 4.24); the community because the temple was impure and used a false calendar. Not every verbal contact between the Gospel and the Scrolls signifies a material connection.

44 Op. cit., p. 217.

45 Ibid., p. 220.

46 Ibid., p. 220.

47 Ibid., p. 221.

48 Cf. p. 40.

49 According to the old tradition the gospel was written in Ephesus. The view (e.g. J. N. Sanders, *The Fourth Gospel in the Early Church* (Cambridge 1943), pp. 38–43) that it was written in Alexandria is not convincing; but certainty is not attainable.

50 Cf. pp. 40–56.

51 Cf. pp. 56ff.

52 Cf. pp. 67f.

53 The book by R. McL. Wilson mentioned in n. 28 offers a good survey.

54 1.18. If one reads θεός instead of υἱός, the argument is still stronger: cf. 3.18.

55 Cf. 1.1. What is said of the Logos may also be said of the Son.

56 See my commentary (London 1955), ad loc.

57 Cf. Rev. 2.9; 3.9.

58 *A Greek–English Lexicon of the New Testament and other Early Christian Literature*, tr. and ed. W. F. Arndt and F. W. Gingrich (Chicago and Cambridge 1957), s.v.

59 In *Theological Dictionary of the New Testament*, tr. and ed. G. W. Bromiley, II (Grand Rapids, Michigan 1964), pp. 509f.

60 *Das Evangelium nach Johannes* (Göttingen 1951), p. 188.

61 πάντας—both heathen and Jew—ἐλκύσω πρὸς ἐμαυτόν.

CHAPTER 2

1 Schuyler Brown, 'From Burney to Black: the Fourth Gospel and the Aramaic Question' in *Catholic Biblical Quarterly* 26 (1964), pp. 323–339.

2 M. Black, *An Aramaic Approach to the Gospels and Acts* (3e., Oxford 1967).

3 S. Brown, op. cit., p. 339.

4 J. Jeremias, *The Central Message of the New Testament* (London 1965), p. 74.

5 Many examples are to be found in the commentaries; a noteworthy list drawn from the Poimandres is given by Dodd, *Interpretation*, p. 34.

6 Cf. 8.38; 17.5.

7 F. C. Burkitt, *Church and Gnosis* (Cambridge 1932), p. 95.

8 Matt. 13.56; 26.18; Mark 4.1; 6.3; 9.19; 14.49; Luke 3.9; 22.56; John 5.45; Acts 12.20; 1 Cor. (2.3); 16.6, 7; 2 Cor. 5.8; 11.9; 12.21; Gal. 4.18, 20; Phil. 1.26; 1 Thess. 3.4; 2 Thess. 2.5; 3.1, 10; 2 John 12. Cf. 1 John 1.2.

9 This second argument is only adduced *ad hominem*. Cf. my commentary, ad loc., and (for the witness of P⁶⁶) my article: 'Papyrus Bodmer II: A Preliminary Report' in *Expository Times* 68 (1956–7), p. 175.

10 Cf. Judg. 13.2 (A): καὶ ἐγένετο ἀνὴρ . . . καὶ ὄνομα αὐτῷ Μανωε (ויהי איש אחד . . . ושמו מנוח); Job 1.1: ἄνθρωπός τις ἦν . . . ᾧ ὄνομα Ιωβ (איש היה . . . איוב שמו).

11 J. H. Bernard, *A Critical and Exegetical Commentary on the Gospel according to St John* (Edinburgh 1928), p. 8.

12 E. C. Colwell, *The Greek of the Fourth Gospel* (Chicago 1931), pp. 34ff.

13 *Greek–English Lexicon* (Oxford 1940), s.v. εἰς, v. 2: 'of Purpose or Object'.

14 Cf. 1.31; 13.18; (14.31); 15.25.

15 The ambiguity of the sentence is perhaps intentional, a possibility I did not consider in the first edition of my commentary. Such ambiguities are characteristic of John.

16 Op. cit., p. 51.

17 Op. cit., pp. 63ff.

18 Cf. 10.18; 19.10, 11; also 7.1, if εἶχεν ἐξουσίαν is to be read there. For ἐξουσία with the infinitive cf. 5.27.

19 N. Turner, *A Grammar of New Testament Greek* by J. H. Moulton III (Edinburgh 1963), p. 27.

20 Therefore this usage is not to be considered a Semitism.

21 Liddell–Scott, s.v.

22 J. H. Moulton, *A Grammar of New Testament Greek* (Edinburgh 1908), p. 147.

23 Or certain elements in biblical Greek.

24 F. Blass and A. Debrunner, *A Greek Grammar of the New Testament and Other Early Christian Literature*, tr. and rev. R. W. Funk (Chicago and London 1961), § 341.

25 τὰς πρώτας αἰεὶ χάριτας . . . ἐπισχὼν καὶ ταμιευσάμενος εἰσαῦθις ἑτέρας ἀντ᾽ ἐκείνων καὶ τρίτας ἀντὶ τῶν δευτέρων καὶ αἰεὶ νέας ἀντὶ παλαιοτέρων . . . ἐπιδίδωσι. The Johannine abbreviation of this form of speech is in no way Semitic.

26 Therefore χάριν ἀντὶ χάριτος is not to be regarded as a translation of חסדא חלף חסדא (M. Black in *Journal of Theological Studies* 42 (1941), pp. 69f); there is no Semitism to be seen here either.

27 Cf. Blass, op. cit., § 205f.

28 Op. cit.

29 Op. cit.

30 K. Beyer, *Semitische Syntax im Neuen Testament* 1.1 (Göttingen 1962).

31 Cf. p. 24.

32 Op. cit., p. 95.

33 Op. cit., p. 280.

34 As in the Syriac translations.

35 Op. cit., p. 192; cf. Turner, op. cit., p. 153.

36 P. 25.

37 'The Religious Background of the Fourth Gospel' in *Studies in the Fourth Gospel*, ed. F. L. Cross (London 1957), pp. 36–44.

38　Kilpatrick is arguing against Dodd.

39　ἐξουσία is especially frequent in the Aramaic portions of the Book of Daniel, usually as a translation of the root שְׁלֵט.

40　In 2 Chron. 22.6 θεᾶσθαι translates רָאָה. It occurs seven times in Tobit, Judith, 2 and 3 Maccabees.

41　See, for example, R. E. Brown, *The Gospel according to John* (i–xii) (Anchor Bible, New York 1966), pp. cxxii–cxxv.

42　See, for example, C. H. Dodd, op. cit., pp. 54–73.

43　L. Koehler and W. Baumgartner, *Lexicon in Veteris Testamenti Libros* (Leiden 1953), s.v. חֶסֶד.

44　R. E. Brown, op. cit., pp. 3f.

45　In my commentary (London 1955), p. 132.

46　The question of the disciples of John is discussed in detail in a Durham dissertation by J. H. Hughes, part of which has now been published in *Novum Testamentum* 14 (1972), pp. 191–218.

47　Many parallels are provided by W. L. Knox, *Some Hellenistic Elements in Primitive Christianity* (London 1944), pp. 55–8.

48　Many believe that the prologue was not written by the evangelist, but was taken up by him and made to fit his purpose. So, for example, R. E. Brown, op. cit., p. 1: 'An early Christian hymn, probably stemming from Johannine circles, which has been adapted to serve as an overture to the Gospel narrative of the career of the incarnate Word'; see also R. Bultmann, *John* (chapter 1, note 25), ad loc.; E. Käsemann, *New Testament Questions of Today*, tr. W. J. Montague (Philadelphia 1969), pp. 138–67. I may now refer to my Ethel M. Wood Lecture, *The Prologue of St John's Gospel* (London 1971, reprinted in *New Testament Essays*, London 1972).

49　M. J. Lagrange, *Évangile selon St Jean* (Paris 1947); R. D. Potter, 'Topography and Archaeology in the Fourth Gospel' in *Studia Evangelica* i (Texte und Untersuchungen 73) (Berlin 1959), pp. 329–337.

50　Even here there may be room for doubt, as E. Haenchen said to me in Münster. The pool of St Anna is a double pool; if the pool John had in mind was a double pool, we hear nothing of this in the Gospel.

51　W. F. Albright, 'Recent Discoveries in Palestine and the Gospel of St John' in *The Background of the New Testament and its Eschatology*, ed. W. D. Davies and D. Daube (Cambridge 1956), pp. 153–71.

52　Op. cit., p. 331.

53 Potter, op. cit., p. 333; Lagrange, op. cit., pp. 92f.

54 Op. cit., p. 159.

55 Op. cit., p. 333.

56 *The Beginnings of Christianity* v (London 1933), p. 485.

57 *Revue Biblique* 42 (1933), pp. 83–113; 59 (1952), pp. 513–30.

58 *Revue Biblique* 59 (1952), pp. 531–50 = *Exégèse et Théologie* (Paris 1961) I, pp. 316–39.

59 Op. cit., p. 159.

60 Naturally, it is possible that the author of a source could have been interested in topographical accuracy.

61 It was my original purpose to deal in this lecture with a third theme, namely, the contention that the framework of the gospel was determined by a Jewish calendar of feasts and lections. But time prevents this. Cf. A. Guilding, *The Fourth Gospel and Jewish Worship* (Oxford 1960), and the reviews of N. H. Snaith in *Journal of Theological Studies* 12 (1961), pp. 322ff; E. Haenchen, *Theologische Literaturzeitung* 86 (1961), columns 670ff; M. E. Boismard, *Revue Biblique* 68 (1961), pp. 599–602; also D. M. Smith, *The Composition and Order of the Fourth Gospel* (Yale Publications in Religion 10, New Haven and London 1965), pp. 102–5.

62 This is not, however, a judgement about the historicity of the gospel.

CHAPTER 3

1 For a detailed discussion see my commentary, pp. 105–14.

2 This influence may be clearly seen in the controversy stories and in the use of messianic titles; cf., for example, Mark 12.35ff.

3 This is a far-reaching question, which obviously can here be answered only in outline form.

4 The translation is from G. H. Box, *The Apocalypse of Abraham* (Translations of Early Documents, London 1918).

5 Ibid., p. 74.

6 Ibid., p. xxi.

7 Cf. the outstanding discussion by W. D. Davies in *Christian Origins and Judaism* (London 1962), pp. 19–30 ('Apocalyptic and Pharisaism'). Davies shows that there is no essential difference between Apocalypticism and Pharisaism, and in this he is certainly right.

He writes (p. 29): 'It is precarious to assume that the exclusion of the Apocalyptic literature from the Canon implied a set hostility to it on their [the rabbis'] part.' Here, however, it is not a matter of hostility; we are concerned only with the fact that in the Old Testament there is only one Apocalypse, and that the time of the flourishing of Jewish Apocalyptic, which began about two hundred years before Christ, had by the period we are considering already ended.

8   Cf. Mark 9.1; 13.30. Since A. Schweitzer the problem has been frequently discussed.

9   Mark 13.2; 14.58; 15.29 and parallels; cf. John 2.19.

10 For example, 6.39, 40, etc. ($\dot{\epsilon}\nu \tau\hat{\eta} \dot{\epsilon}\sigma\chi\acute{a}\tau\eta \dot{\eta}\mu\acute{\epsilon}\rho\alpha$). This and similar verses may be interpolations, but they are a significant part of the gospel as we read it today. See below, pp. 73f.

11 For example, Johanan ben Zakkai; cf. the following.

12 Cf. p. 73f.

13 F. C. Burkitt, *Jewish and Christian Apocalypses* (London 1914), p. 12.

14 See Strack–Billerbeck I, p. 468.

15 J. Neusner, *A Life of Rabban Yohanan ben Zakkai* (2e., Leiden 1970), p. 180.

16 W. D. Davies (op. cit., p. 23) writes: 'R. Johanan b. Zakkai (first century A.D.) was so convinced of the speedy appearance of the Messiah that he modified his ordinances regulating a certain religious ceremony in view of this expectation (*T. B. Rosh ha-Shanah*, 30a), and in *T. B. Berakhoth* 29b, it is confirmed that he expected the Messiah in the near future.' Berakhoth 29b is an error for 28b, a rather obscure passage (cf. Strack–Billerbeck II, pp. 335f), which one may only use with caution. In *Rosh ha-Shanah* 30a (actually Mishnah *R. ha-Shanah* 4.3) there appears the following passage: 'Beforetime the *Lulab* was carried seven days in the Temple, but in the provinces one day only. After the Temple was destroyed Rabban Johanan b. Zakkai ordained that in the provinces it should be carried seven days in memory of the Temple (זכר למקדש)' (Danby's translation). This passage manifests a wish to commemorate the past rather than to nurture a hope for the future (one may compare in the New Testament the position of Luke).

17 Neusner, op. cit., p. 183.

18 Ed. Schechter 34a.

19 Op. cit., p. 184.

20 There is a corresponding individualism in the Fourth Gospel; see
    C. F. D. Moule, 'The Individualism of the Fourth Gospel' in
    Novum Testamentum 5 (1962), pp. 171–90. A thoroughgoing com-
    parison between John and Johanan would prove rewarding.

21 Cf. Strack–Billerbeck I, p. 878.

22 It is possible that the effect of the military collapse in the year 70
    has been somewhat overestimated. K. W. Clark, 'Worship in the
    Jerusalem Temple after A.D. 70' in *New Testament Studies* 6 (1960),
    pp. 269–80, attempted to show that the temple worship did not end
    completely at this time. On the whole his argument is convincing.
    It remains doubtful, however, whether the continuing use of the
    temple, which was certainly insignificant, can explain the dying out
    of apocalyptic.

23 For example, Brown (pp. lxxxv, 380); Barrett (pp. 299f). On this
    subject compare the article of E. Lerle, 'Liturgische Reformen des
    Synagogengottesdienstes als Antwort auf die judenchristliche Mis-
    sion des ersten Jahrhunderts' in *Novum Testamentum* 10 (1968), pp.
    31–42.

24 Mart. Pol. 13.1 (... μάλιστα Ἰουδαίων προθύμως, ὡς ἔθος αὐτοῖς);
    cf. 12.2; 17.2; 18.1.

25 J. Jocz, *The Jewish People and Jesus Christ* (London 1949), pp. 56f.

26 The word ἀποσυνάγωγος recalls the different forms of the syna-
    gogue ban; see Strack–Billerbeck IV, pp. 293–333.

27 It is also worth noting that the use of the expression אני הוא is per-
    haps just as closely related to the Johaninne ἐγώ εἰμι as other
    expressions which are more frequently cited.

28 Especially if we follow those haggada texts in which the word has
    the article (השליח). The article appears also in some texts of the
    Mekilta on Exod. 12.12; admittedly this is not the reading that
    usually appears. The Mekilta passage runs: שומע אני על ידי מלאך או
    על ידי שליח תלמוד לומר (Exod. 12. 29) ויי הכה כל בכור לא על
    ידי מלאך ולא על ידי שליח. This passage and that in the haggada are
    not identical. It is probable that both attest the presence of the
    Jewish Christian mission and different forms of necessary counter-
    measures.

29 The passage runs as follows: Rab Judah (†299) said, Samuel (†254)
    said, In the surrounding country too [as well as in the temple] they
    sought to recite thus [i.e., with the Ten Commandments before the
    Shema], but they had already abolished them because of the

complaining (or, slander) of the Minim. Again, it was taught [a Baraita]: R. Nathan (*c.* 160) said, In the surrounding country too they sought to recite thus, but they had already abolished them because of the complaining (or, slander) of the Minim. Rabbah bar bar Ḥanah (*c.* 280) thought to establish it in Sura; Rab Ḥisda said to him, They have already abolished them because of the complaining (or, slander) of the Minim. Amemar (*c.* 400) thought to establish it In Nᵉhardᵉ‘a; Rab Ashi (†427) said to him, They have already abolished them because of the complaining (or, slander) of the Minim. I have taken the dates from Strack–Billerbeck IV, p. 191.

30 A. Schlatter, *Geschichte Israels von Alexander dem Grossen bis Hadrian* (3e., Stuttgart 1925), p. 373; also H. Bietenhard, *Soṭa* (Giessener Mischna) (Berlin 1956), pp. 165f.

31 'Der Dialog ist . . . zwischen 155 und 160 ausgearbeitet worden; aber er versetzt uns . . . in die Zeit um 135 und verarbeitet, was Justin damals in Ephesus erlebt hat.' So wrote A. Harnack, *Die Chronologie der altchristlichen Literatur bis Eusebius* I (Leipzig 1897), p. 281.

32 *The Apostolic Fathers* II 1 (London 1885).

33 In *Handbuch zum Neuen Testament: Ergänzungsband* (Tübingen 1920).

34 Th. Zahn, *Geschichte des Neutestamentlichen Kanons* I (Erlangen 1888), p. 846; II (Erlangen und Leipzig 1890), pp. 945–8.

35 Op. cit., p. 260.

36 Or perhaps: 'I am no believer.'

37 See also *Magnesians* 8, 9; *Philadelphians* 9; *Smyrnaeans* 5, 7.

38 See below, pp. 69ff.

39 Cf. 1 John 2.20; also 1 Cor. 8.1.

40 An important exception is Virginia Corwin, *St Ignatius and Christianity in Antioch* (Yale Publications in Religion I) (New Haven 1960), pp. 52–65, who traces at least three groups in Antioch.

41 'The testimony of history thus agrees with that of the coins. . . . It is in this sense that I consider it certain that Khirbet Qumran was destroyed by the Romans in June 68 of our era.' So R. de Vaux, *L'Archéologie et les manuscrits de la mer morte* (London 1961), pp. 32f; for a different view see G. R. Driver, *The Judean Scrolls* (Oxford 1965), pp. 394–9.

42 On the possibility that members of the Qumran community went over to the Christian church, see below, p. 68.

43 For example, 'Die in Palästina gefundenen hebräischen Texte und das Neue Testament' in *Zeitschrift für Theologie und Kirche* 47 (1950), pp. 192–211; 'Die Sektenschrift und die iranische Religion' in *Zeitschrift für Theologie und Kirche* 49 (1952), pp. 296–316; 'Die Schriftrollen vom Toten Meer und ihre Bedeutung' in *Universitas* 12 (1957), pp. 121–30.

44 Especially in *Qumran und das Neue Testament* (Tübingen 1966).

45 'The Qumran Scrolls and the Johannine Gospel and Epistles' in *The Scrolls and the New Testament* (New York 1957; London 1958), pp. 183–207. Cf. now also his commentary on John (New York 1966, and 1970).

46 See now especially J. H. Charlesworth, ed., *John and Qumran* (London 1972).

47 See my article in *The Cambridge History of the Bible* I (Cambridge 1970), pp. 377–411.

48 G. R. Driver, op. cit., pp. 168–225.

CHAPTER 4

1 C. C. Torrey, *The Four Gospels: A new Translation* (London 1933); *Our Translated Gospels* (London n.d.); also 'The Aramaic Period of the Nascent Christian Church' in *Zeitschrift für die neutestamentliche Wissenschaft* 44 (1952/53), pp. 205–23.

2 C. F. Burney, *The Aramaic Origin of the Fourth Gospel* (Oxford 1922).

3 Cf. above, p. 35.

4 See p. 36, n. 51; also *The Archaeology of Palestine* (Harmondsworth 1949), pp. 244–8.

5 W. Temple, *Readings in St John's Gospel* (London 1945), p. xix.

6 Ibid., p. xx.

7 C. K. Barrett, 'The Theological Vocabulary of the Fourth Gospel and of the Gospel of Truth' in *Current Issues in New Testament Interpretation: Essays in Honour of Otto A. Piper*, ed. W. Klassen and G. F. Snyder (New York and London 1962), pp. 210–23.

8 This statement should not be understood as a defence of the historicity of the Johannine narratives, nor as an assertion of the view that John intended to attack Docetism. Yet I cannot agree with Käsemann in the view that John manifests a 'naive Docetism' (*The*

Testament of Jesus, tr. G. Krodel (Philadelphia 1968), p. 26 and elsewhere), except in the sense that he has not successfully brought his faith in the historical character of the activity of Jesus into agreement with his divine sonship. But the Chalcedonian Fathers were also unable to do that!

9 Since they are the deeds of a 'God walking upon the earth' (Käsemann, loc. cit.) and therefore not only historical but also eternal. This paradox is unavoidable in any gospel in which the evangelist does not use his material as pure allegory; but it is particularly sharp in the Fourth Gospel.

10 R. Bultmann, *ThWbNT* i (1933), pp. 711ff.

11 Bultmann correctly notes that knowledge in the Old Testament indicates a relation between subject and object, but in Gnosis is speculative. That means: 'Da γινώσκειν also die Annahme der Liebestat Gottes in Jesus und den Gehorsam gegen seine Forderung bedeutet, könnte es scheinen, dass das johanneische γινώσκειν dem at.lichen ידע entspricht. Aber so gewiss der johanneische Erkenntnisbegriff dem at.lichen verwandt ist, so tritt doch die Eigenart des johanneischen Denkens erst ganz hervor, wenn man sieht, dass γινώσκειν gerade nicht das at.liche ידע, sondern in paradoxer Umprägung das hellenistisch-gnostische γινώσκειν aufnimmt' (p. 712). But this is scarcely convincing. Recently this difficult question has been excellently treated in an as yet unpublished dissertation by J. Painter.

12 Pp. 59f.

13 Pp. 2f.

14 Pp. 8–11.

15 R. H. Lightfoot, *St John's Gospel* (Oxford 1956), pp. 32f.

16 See p. 2, n. 10.

17 Op. cit., p. 73.

18 Ibid., p. 96.

19 Or to Gnosis. Cf. p. 6, n. 28.

20 Cf. pp. 6f.

21 Especially C. Colpe, *Die religionsgeschichtliche Schule* (Göttingen 1961).

22 P. 58.

23 C. K. Barrett, *Jesus and the Gospel Tradition* (London 1967), pp. 48, 105–8.

24 The expectation of the parousia continued throughout the entire second century and even longer (cf., for example, Ignatius, Papias, Justin, Irenaeus). Although a formal hope for the parousia, indeed for an imminent parousia, remained lively, it was necessarily altered. The first century and the expectation of the arrival of the Son of man within the first generation could not be repeated.

25 Paul had to struggle against Judaizing institutionalism and an early Gnosticism—occasionally in the same persons. Cf. E. Käsemann, *Exegetische Versuche und Besinnungen* 1 (Göttingen 1960), p. 178.

26 Philo, for example, insisted upon the literal sense of the Law and at the same time showed Gnostic tendencies.

27 Cf. T. F. Torrance, *The Doctrine of Grace in the Apostolic Fathers* (Edinburgh and London 1948).

28 P. 47, n. 22.

29 Cf. W. Bauer, *Orthodoxy and Heresy in Earliest Christianity*, tr. and ed. R. A. Kraft and G. Krodel *et al.* (Philadelphia 1971), p. 67.

30 E. Käsemann, 'New Testament Questions of Today' in *New Testament Questions of Today*, p. 21.

31 In 'Paul and Early Catholicism' (*New Testament Questions of Today*, p. 237) Käsemann defines early Catholicism in a different way: 'Early catholicism means that transition from earliest Christianity to the so-called ancient Church, which is completed with the disappearance of the imminent expectation. This by no means occurs everywhere at the same time or with the same consequences, but nevertheless in the various streams there is a characteristic movement toward that great Church which understands itself as the *Una Sancta Apostolica.*' Since Gnosticism could arise in response to the disappearance of the expectation of the imminent parousia, there is a possibility of a gnosticizing early Catholicism.

32 Cf. J. Abelson, *The Immanence of God in Rabbinical Literature* (London 1912), especially pp. 340–56.

33 Pp. 51–5.

34 'Die neuentdeckten Qumrantexte und das Judenchristentum der Pseudoklementinen' in *Neutestamentliche Studien für R. Bultmann* (Berlin 1954), pp. 35–51.

35 Ibid., p. 51.

36 *Dialogue* 47: σωθήσεται ὁ τοιοῦτος (a Jewish Christian), ἐὰν μὴ τοὺς ἄλλους ἀνθρώπους (Gentile Christians) . . . ἐκ παντὸς πείθειν

ἀγωνίζηται ταὐτὰ αὐτῷ φυλάσσειν. Doubtless some Jewish Christians had attempted to do this.

37 Pp. 47f.

38 Tos. Ḥullin 2.22f: It happened that a snake bit R. El'azar b. Dama (*c.* 130). There came Ja'qob from Kephar-Sama, in order to heal him in the name of Yeshua' b. Panṭera; but R. Ishma'el . . . did not allow him. It was said to him: That you may not do, ben Dama. He answered R. Ishma'el: I want to bring you the proof, that he may heal me. He had, however, not brought the proof when he died. R. Ishma'el said: Well for you, ben Dama, that you have departed in peace without having broken the ordinance of the scholars; since in the end judgement overtakes anyone who breaks through the fence of the scholars; see Eccles. 10.8 (Whoso breaketh through a fence, a serpent shall bite him). See Strack–Billerbeck I, p. 36.

39 Tos. Ḥullin 2.24: (R. Eli'ezer could not understand why he was brought before the tribunal and accused of heresy.) R. Aqiba (†*c.* 135) came to him and said: Rabbi, I should like to say something in your presence; perhaps you will not be annoyed. He said to him: Say on! He said to him: Perhaps one of the heretics said a word of heresy to you, and it pleased you. He answered: By heaven, there you awaken a memory in me! Once I went out on a street of Sepphoris; there I encountered Ja'aqob of Kephar-Sikhnim, who spoke a word of heresy in the name of Yeshua' ben Panṭera, and it pleased me, and I was arrested on account of the heresy, because I had overstepped the words of the Torah (Prov. 5.8; 7.26). See Strack–Billerbeck I, p. 37.

40 Pp. 51–6.

41 For example, Rom. 9—11; I. Cor. 10.1–13; 2 Cor. 3.4–18; Gal. 4.21–31.

42 R. E. Brown, op. cit., pp. lvii–lxiv.

43 P. Winter, *On the Trial of Jesus* (Berlin 1961).

44 It is of course possible to ascribe these references to a last day to an ecclesiastical redactor. But (*a*) it is the task of exegesis to explain the text as it is, and (*b*) the interweaving of present and future cannot be explained in every passage by literary analysis; see, for example, 11.25f.

45 Such concepts as Son of man (heavenly Man), Messiah, resurrection, and the last day are to be found not only in the synoptic tradition, but also in the Pauline letters. Without them the early Christians could not have expressed their faith.

46 It is not a matter of maintaining that any source or redaction hypothesis must be wrong. The gospel as we read it today has doubtless been put together from sources by means of redaction, and therefore source and redaction analysis can be practised with profit. I maintain only that the redactor was a theologian, not a fool.

47 Op. cit., pp. 98–104. Also here (cf. nn. 44, 46) it is entirely legitimate to speak of sources and redaction, if only a source or redaction hypothesis is not made a substitute for exegesis. On this subject cf. E. Lohse, 'Wort und Sakrament im Johannesevangelium' in *New Testament Studies* 7 (1961), pp. 110–25.

48 John 'poses for us the riddle of whether he was a heretic or a genuine witness' (E. Käsemann, *Exegetische Versuche und Besinnungen* i (Göttingen) 1960), p. 187). To accept the word 'heretic' means, as I see it, to play into the hands of Diotrephes, whose intention is to categorize Christians as heretics or as orthodox. Perhaps it would be better to call John 'witness and nonconformist' rather than 'heretic and witness'.

49 The Old Testament contains a law, to be sure, but speaks also of the love of God, which is without legal conditions. It requires a sacrificial cult, to be sure, but goes on to declare that the offerings as such are worthless. For rabbinic Judaism see the well-known passage Aboth 3.16 (Danby): All is foreseen, but freedom of choice is given; and the world is judged by grace, yet all is according to the excess of works (לפי רוב המעשה) [that be good or evil]. Cf. Josephus, *Bell.* 2.162f; *Ant.* 13.172; 18.13. See now G. Maier, *Mensch und freier Wille nach den jüdischen Religionsparteien zwischen Ben Sira und Paulus* (Tübingen 1971).

50 The complete separation between church and synagogue became the model for the division between free Gnosis and hardened orthodoxy and for that between ecclesiastical office and spiritual power. All these divisions have been unfortunate, but the first was perhaps the most unfortunate.

51 Cf. E. Grässer, 'Die antijüdische Polemik im Johannesevangelium' in *New Testament Studies* 11 (1964), pp. 74–90.

Index of Authors Cited

Index of Passages Cited

NON-BIBLICAL PASSAGES

CHRISTIAN WRITERS